FROM THERE TO HERE

FROM THERE TO HERE

WAR, PEACE, PANDEMIC

A Memoir by Romy Wyllie

ISBN 978-0-578-76968-4
eISBN 978-0-578-77747-4

Library of Congress Control Number:
2020919915

IngramSpark Publishers
Printing by Lightning Source International, USA

Book Design by James Alexander of Jade Design
(www.jadedesign.co.uk)

Cover design: The typography is reminiscent of
the 1940s KEEP CALM posters. The photograph
of Romy was taken at age 5 or 6 just before war
was declared. The planes in the background are
Hurricanes, heroes of the Battle of Britain.

To Pete

My beloved husband for 64 years and on

PREFACE

March 11, 2020: the World Health Organization (WHO) declared the coronavirus outbreak a pandemic, meaning that the COVID-19 disease will spread to all countries on the globe. Numbers of deceased change daily with the United States having the dubious distinction of surpassing totals recorded by any other country.

With scientists and medical experts speculating about the consequences of this global pandemic, we recognize that we are at war, not with another nation or nations but with a virus to which we have no immunity nor a vaccine for protection. As the crisis hits us and new restrictions are imposed daily on our normal existence, I am reminded of the many travails of World War II and how we overcame them. During that time, a common saying was *for the duration,* a phrase meaning the end of something and originally used during World War I to describe the terms of enlistment for several years, or for the duration of that war.

MARCH 19, 2020: the Governor of California ordered everyone to stay at home to slow the spread of the virus. Only the most essential businesses, such as supermarkets and drugstores, were allowed to operate. Most other states did the same. The economic fallout has been devastating as all commerce, especially small operations, face unimaginable hardships.

My husband of 64 years has just turned 90 and I am 87. At present we are healthy and active. While keeping our distance from others, we have continued to exercise to strengthen our immune systems. My Jazzercise class is being streamed through Facebook; I have increased my walking days; and continue to play tennis on a private court. But with all public gathering places closed, there was suddenly a large gap in our lives. To fill that void, I decided to write this book recalling my childhood growing up in the midst of daily and nightly air raids, and innumerable restrictions and rationing affecting our lives. Set against the backdrop of World War II, the book chronicles what I can remember of my early life from birth to marriage to a three-year stay in America, creating a prequel to *Loving Andrew: a Fifty-Two-Year Story of Down Syndrome* which was published in 2012.

I have found inspiration and detailed information on the early years of World War II in Erik Larson's *The Splendid and the Vile* which "takes readers out of today's political dysfunction and back to a time of true leadership, when—in the face of unrelenting horror—Churchill's eloquence, courage, and perseverance bound a country, and a family, together." Larson's book brings home one important difference between today's social distancing and World War II's public gatherings. In order to reduce the spread of COVID-19, concerts, meetings, classes, plays and church services were cancelled; schools, restaurants, bars, clubs, gyms and businesses were closed. During the second World War's devastating Blitz of London and other major cities, gathering spots and shops remained open. In London the working classes gathered in pubs and the upper classes congregated in restaurants and nightclubs. Even the famous debutante presentations at

Grosvenor House continued during an air raid on March 8, 1941. Larson explained that some of the guests planned to carry on partying afterwards at the famous Café de Paris, only to discover that a German bomb had destroyed the Café in spite of its basement location. Undeterred, the guests went on to another nightclub where they danced and drank until the next morning. It was this defiance against all odds that helped both rich and poor sustain their fighting spirit.

May 8, 2020 was the 75th anniversary of VE day which marked the end of the war in Europe. In England the Red Arrows flew in a V-formation over London with red, white and blue smoke trailing across the sky behind them. Standing in a green meadow near the edge of the Dover cliffs, a lone piper, in the Royal Stewart kilt of the Scots Guards, played a mournful refrain as two Spitfires flew low, dipping and turning, over the iconic white cliffs. It was especially poignant to compare news clips from 1945 of large crowds singing and dancing in the streets and squares of London with current pictures of those same gathering places now devoid of people, due to the coronavirus lockdown.

Encouraged by Winston Churchill's indomitable leadership, we put up with the conditions and restrictions, confident that the war would end. At the start of the pandemic, columnist Steve Lopez of the Los Angeles Times reminded us that "this too shall pass." We shall eventually see light at the end of the tunnel and hopefully survive this dark time with the help of activities that can be pursued in the safety of home. Therefore, I have put pen to paper, or fingers to keyboard, to write a memoir entitled: *From There to Here: War, Peace, Pandemic.*

CHILDHOOD

I. THE LAND OF GREEN GINGER

You are grown, and your children are grown,
and you live very far from
The Land of Green Ginger Street,
but still in a mutable world,
where possibility comes
from the second nature of things.
—Robin Richstone

A little girl, aged four or five, wearing a pretty flowered dress with a bow decorating her hair, sits alone at the bottom of a long flight of steps. Her expression is one of puzzlement and concern. Is she wondering how to climb up all those steps? Does the steep staircase symbolize the future challenges of her journey through life? Where are the people who take care of her? Can she see her mother or her nanny among the group of grown-ups and two large golden retrievers milling around on the lawn below? At present a peaceful world of adventure awaits her, but there are dark clouds looming on the horizon, soon to affect her life and leave a scar on her memory forever. This is her story.

My Mother, Mary Blair, with me as a baby

I was born in England on November 6, 1932, in Kingston-upon-Hull commonly called Hull, a town situated on the River Hull at its confluence with the Humber Estuary, 25 miles inland from the North Sea. For many centuries this ideal location had made Hull an important port city: a center for trade, a fishing and whaling center, a market town, and an industrial metropolis. My name is Frances Rosemary Blair; my mother called me Rosemary, but my father shortened my middle name to Romy. Both my maternal grandmother and my mother were Frances Harriet Woodhouse and Frances Mary Blair respectively, and both were known by their middle names. I had three brothers: George Herbert Blair eight years older, John Woodhouse Blair six years older, and Robert (Bob) David Blair eight years younger—all known by their first names.

When I was born, my parents lived in a respectable, ivy-covered house called Westwood, across from a park on the edge of the city. My father, who was born in Scotland, was a surgeon with a successful practice. He was appointed Assistant Surgeon at Hull Royal Infirmary in September 1919, and full Surgeon in May 1923, eventually becoming Senior Surgeon, a position that he held until his retirement in August 1947 when he was made Honorary Consulting Surgeon.

My mother was one of six children—five girls and one boy—born to Herbert and Frances Harriet Woodhouse. My maternal grandfather, Herbert Woodhouse, was a solicitor with offices on a street whimsically called The Land of Green Ginger, a narrow road at the bottom of Whitefriargate in the old town of Hull. The name of the street conjures up visions of Far Eastern cities with their crowded souks and merchants calling in Middle Eastern languages for shoppers to view their colorful and aromatic displays of spices. Although some writers have ascertained that the name of the street is a corruption of a Dutch family surname *Lindegren jonger* (Lindegreen junior), or a memory of *Landgrave Granger*, a pathway leading to the home of the Landgrave family, I prefer to think that it is a reference to the root ginger which, when cured with lemon juice, becomes an exotic spice. Spices were certainly among the many commodities imported up the River Hull. Based on the discovery during a recent excavation of a large number of wooden crates in an underground chamber, spices may have been stored below one or more of the buildings bordering the Land of Green Ginger street.

On learning that my grandfather had offices on a street with such a romantic name, Robin Richstone, a poet and friend of mine wrote the following:

The Land of Green Ginger Street—for Romy.

When you walked down this English street,
a small blond child, you could see
visions, stacks of white sail
looming up from a harbor
stuffed with mysteries
to be traded for ordinary things.
Plain shillings turned into wild spices,
fine leaves and berries that burn the tongue,
silk cool on the skin,
by means of a long and patient passage.
You are grown, and your children are grown,

and you live very far from

The Land of Green Ginger Street,

but still in a mutable world,

where possibility comes

from the second nature of things.

The poem encapsulates my life: a young girl grows up and moves far away from her family's link to an oddly-named street. She holds the name in her memory and one day shares it with a friend.

My father, Robert Bertram Blair, was born on August 15, 1887, in Markinch, Fife, Scotland, to John Blair and Jessie Louden. He was one of eleven children, six girls and five boys. Two children died in infancy, and one accidentally drowned at age 13. Only three members married and had children. My grandfather, John Blair, inherited his father's successful tailoring business and lived to be 75. His wife, however, died at the age of 44, and a cousin, Agnes, came to live with the Markinch Blairs on the death of her own parents and helped bring up the motherless children.

My father's youngest sister, Florence, became a close and constant friend to all of us. She became the link holding together the Blair family as they went their various ways. She was a teacher and dedicated Rotarian. She recorded the family tree, took an interest in all of us, and loved to meet family members of all ages.

Two of the boys, my father and his older brother George, studied medicine at Edinburgh University. My father also attended the Royal College of Surgeons, Edinburgh. Along with their brother Edward, they fought in World War I. Edward was killed in action, but George and my father survived. Except for what I have read of the horrendous conditions and huge loss of life in WWI, I know little of my father's experiences because he never talked about them. He was a Major in the Royal Army Medical Corps and surgical specialist to the British Expeditionary Force in France, devoting most of his attention to limb surgery. I have photos of him in his dress uniform and on horseback. I know that he was gassed and suffered, along with all the other soldiers, from the wet and muddy conditions of the trenches. His job was just behind the front lines helping to treat and rescue the wounded. He brought back not only nightmarish memories but a few mementos of the fighting. When he died my mother discovered two revolvers in his underwear drawer: a regulation officer's pistol and a German revolver. He also brought home other souvenirs: a row of brass-tipped bullets lined the hearth in our family sitting room. Every week our dedicated maids polished the tips. Only when we moved to a smaller house did my mother discover that there was still powder in the bullets which could have exploded if an ember from the fireplace had hit them.

So many soldiers were killed during WWI that there was a shortage of men, creating a gender gap by over a million. Only three of my father's six sisters and only my mother and two of her four sisters married. My mother, born in 1898, was originally engaged to a young man who was killed during the war. While her fiancé and most men were away, Mummy contributed to the war effort by helping out on a farm. At the end of the war, when her role on the farm was no longer needed, the owner, a titled lady, gave her a beautiful ivory dressing table set: two hairbrushes, two clothes brushes, a mirror, and a shoe horn. I now own that set. On the underside of the hair brush handles are the names of the two cows that Mummy milked, *Bravo* and *Darkie*.

Mummy's eldest sister, Dorothy, born in 1892, fell in love with a married officer who could never divorce his mentally ill wife. But Dorothy followed him on his assignment to Egypt, where she found a job teaching dancing to King Farouk's children. Having adjusted to the warm climate of the Middle East, she spent the rest of her life there enjoying the company of other ex-patriots. Aunt Dorothy was my godmother. On one of her infrequent trips back to England, I met her for tea—I was a college student at the time—and tried in vain to encourage her to talk about her life in Egypt. I wanted to know more about this exotic country with its long history and antiquities, and the kind of life that my aunt led as a single English woman. Because Dorothy had left England to follow her soldier friend—we never found out if they were actually lovers—she probably felt that it was inappropriate to say anything to a young niece.

My mother's other two older sisters married and had a daughter each. Aunt Elsie's marriage ended in tragedy when her husband died of appendicitis in Africa, leaving Elsie with a young baby. Elsie came home from Africa with her baby, Diana, to live near her parents who discouraged her from socializing and leading a normal life, resulting in a depression so severe that she made several attempts to take her own life. Hospitalization led to an irreversible lobotomy and subsequent inability to live on her own. Mother's youngest sister, Constance (Aunt Connie) remained a spinster living at home and looking after her aging parents. Gerald, the eldest child and only boy, studied law and became a junior partner in his father's practice until he was banished from Hull and from any contact with the family after his homosexual activities were revealed. He spent the rest of his life in London. Granny would combine a shopping expedition to Harrods, London's renowned department store, with visits to her beloved son. On Gerald's death we learned that after paying off some of his gay friend's mortgages he had left the balance of his money to be divided between his nephews and nieces.

My maternal grandparents lived in a sizeable house in Cottingham outside Hull, where Mother would take me for tea. Granny was extremely deaf, making it hard to have a conversation. I took piano lessons for many years and loved the chance to play on their baby grand, wishing they would give it to my parents to take a place of honor in our elegant lounge. Sometimes, when we were six or seven, I had a chance to have fun with my cousin, Diana, who lived nearby and whose mother was Aunt Elsie. Diana and I had make-believe tea parties and played in a musty smelling summer house where a wonderful old wooden rocking horse resided.

My grandparents also had an estate in Danes Dyke, near Flamborough Head, a chalk headland with sheer white cliffs, significant for their geology and the nesting site of many seabirds and now a nature reserve. We always thought that Danes Dyke was named for an invasion by the Danes, but it was actually constructed to defend nearby lands to the east, and had its origin in prehistoric times with excavated Bronze Age arrowheads as proof. Here my grandparents spent holidays or long weekends. The house was surrounded by beautiful gardens and lawns sloping down to a densely wooded area with narrow paths leading down to the headland with its pebble beach. Carrying a bucket, spade, and folding stool, my nanny would take me to the stony beach being careful not to trip over exposed roots as we wound our way down the woodland path.

My father, who was 11 years older than my mother, was a handsome man of average height. He had dark hair and a face distinguished by a large nose. He spoke with a soft Scottish lilt that became stronger on the telephone. His outward formality contrasted with a wry sense of humor and a gentleness that made him especially appealing to his patients. Like most of his contemporaries he smoked cigarettes. In the evening while unwinding from the pressures of his medical work, he lit a pipe to accompany his nightcap of good Scotch whisky. To celebrate his success as a leading surgeon, my father decided to move out of the city and purchase a larger house for his growing family. I was three when, in 1935, my parents bought a Georgian mansion, called Kirk Ella House. Until the age of 18, this was the luxurious setting of my childhood. Kirk Ella is a village in the East Riding of Yorkshire about five miles from the center of Hull, on its western edge. It had been a village since the 11th century but only became noteworthy in the 18th and 19th centuries when Hull merchants decided to move out of the city center. Kirk Ella House faces Church Lane which meanders down from The Church of St. Andrew, the focal point of the village with a square tower dating to the mid 15th century.

My childhood home was made up of a main house built in 1798, and a coach house added in 1799, the latter of which

Kirk Ella House garden façade

was converted into an attached garage large enough for four cars. Current real estate advertisements describe the house as "stucco and painted brick with stone dressings and graduated Westmorland slate roof." It had two stories and a full attic originally used as servants' bedrooms. Even in my younger years, I remember my older brothers bemoaning the fact that my parents had hired an architect who *modernized* the house in the process of making necessary improvements. Now, as someone experienced in interior design and an author of books on architectural history, I feel especially sad that many of the significant Georgian features, such as a pedimented front porch and a graceful curving staircase, were removed.

Many years later in 1974, when my husband Pete and I and our three children were visiting England, we stopped to look at Kirk Ella House. Pete felt too embarrassed to ring the doorbell unannounced and stayed in the car, but I was much bolder. With two of our three children in tow, I rang the bell and explained who I was and the purpose of my visit to the owner. The lady was most gracious and let us walk around the house and garden. I was thrilled to see that she and her husband had restored several of the original features of the house.

During my parents' 1935 renovation, one important improvement was stripping the exterior of its Virginia creeper revealing white stucco walls and a staggered three-part façade facing south. At the west end a curving main bay had a central window over three full-height windows opening onto the garden. The center bay had an upper arched window with a border of stained-glass over a porch originally supported by double columns. At the east end a flagstone terrace bordered four more full-height windows with matching sash windows above. During the modernization, all these full-height Georgian windows were replaced with French doors. The second-floor master bedroom was lit by two windows with intricate wrought-iron balconies which were attached in 1873 when the Czarevitch, later Czar Alexander III, father of Nicholas II, the last and ill-fated Romanoff ruler, stayed at the house. The Czarevitch came to inspect a yacht that the then owner of Kirk Ella House, Sir James Reed, was building for him. It was decided to install the balconies so that the Czarevitch could view the gardens. A less likely version claimed that the purpose of the balconies was to allow a guard to watch for assassins and provide an escape through the gardens. I remember occasionally daring to raise the heavy sash window and step on one of the balconies but standing there and looking down on the flagstone terrace below didn't feel safe. During World War II, the government found it necessary to commandeer all available iron and wrought-iron for use as scrap metal for munitions. Local authorities went to private residences, businesses, and parks cutting off iron railings at the base. The stubs that were left behind can still be seen in many places, especially outside buildings in London where they have never been replaced. When they came to Kirk Ella House, they removed some iron railings that bordered a curving flower bed facing the garage in the front of the house. Fortunately, no one inspected the garden side, so the Czarevitch balconies survived, continuing to add historical significance to the house. The origin of the balconies was recorded on a brass plaque that hung above the fireplace in the bedroom. Now there is an additional Heritage Trail plaque on the outside marking the event.

The front door opened onto a large hall with cloakroom and a storage room, which we always referred to as Mother's box room, where she arranged flowers and kept numerous boxes and trunks. I can still see the large porcelain sink and draining board where Mummy cut the flower stems and filled large crystal vases and pottery bowls with an array of colorful blooms to place around the house. The south or garden side of the house consisted of a magnificent drawing room with a marble fireplace. On either side of the fireplace were windows framed by arched alcoves. Glass-fronted cabinets containing pottery figurines had been installed into the outside corners of the alcoves. Across the hall a cozy study led into a paneled dining room. During our residence, the dining room was furnished with beautiful antiques: an oval-shaped Jacobean oak dining table that seated twelve; a double-doored 18th century corner cabinet with a fluted header and implied pilasters on each side matching fluted pilasters that framed a wall shelf. The shelf, which held a collection of pewter plates and mugs, hung over a dresser made in the workshop of the renowned London cabinet-maker Thomas Chippendale born in Otley, Yorkshire in 1718. On a wall facing the windows stood a 17th century linen-press, a cabinet where linens were stored with a press that could be screwed tight to hold them flat. Covering the oak-planked floor below the dining table and matching chairs was a large oriental rug with a bell underneath so Daddy could press it with his foot and ring for the parlor maid to take away the dirty plates and serve the next course. The Jacobean dining table, chairs, corner cabinet, Yorkshire dresser, wall shelf, and pewter collection now adorn the dining room in our California home, bringing back many memories, especially at Christmastime.

Across from Mother's box room was a servant's sitting room, narrow butler's pantry with glass-fronted cabinets, a large kitchen with two adjacent storage areas, and a passageway leading to the boiler and laundry room opening onto a kitchen garden. As a young girl, I enjoyed going to the servants' sitting room and chatting with them. This and the kitchen were the places where Mummy would meet with our cook to plan the weekly menus and find out what foods needed to be purchased.

A month before Christmas, we had a tradition that everyone in the house would help to stir the plum pudding that Edith, the cook, prepared. Small silver trinkets, like a sixpence, a thimble, or a ring were wrapped in wax paper and mixed in with the fruit, leading to great excitement if your serving of pudding at Christmas dinner contained one of the treasures. Edith, a warm, plump woman, was an excellent cook and was especially good at baking cakes and desserts. She used a large coal-burning Aga cooker that stood in its own alcove on one side of the kitchen.

On the second floor were a master suite, with bedroom, lavatory, dressing room and bathroom, three bedrooms and full bath, a servants' wing with two bedrooms and bath, and, up a short flight of stairs, a nursery suite with bedroom and day nursery. We closed off the original servants' bedrooms in the attic although the area remained accessible for necessary maintenance. When some work was being done in the attic, I climbed up the step ladder and looked through the trap door into the space, but most of the wood flooring had been removed making it too dangerous to explore.

I seldom visited my parents' bedroom suite, but I do recall an intriguing glass cabinet that sat on the top of a tall chest of drawers in Daddy's dressing room. The cabinet contained a collection of blown birds' eggs that he had collected as a young boy. One day I asked Daddy to take it down so I could look at the eggs

Kirk Ella House – main lawn with Blair family cricket game

more closely. In the process one of the eggs broke. Daddy took the accident in stride, but I felt guilty for asking to touch them.

I remember the gardens as exceptionally beautiful, intriguing and endless. There were four acres in total with the main formal gardens bordered by high brick walls. Stretching down from the house was a long green lawn, sometimes used for croquet or cricket and terminating in a grass tennis court. The lawn was framed with large trees on either side: cedars of Lebanon, various pine trees, a copper beech tree, a Monkey Puzzle tree (a hardy evergreen native to parts of Chile and Argentina), and a walnut tree, which produced an abundant harvest of nuts. The copper beech tree had a rock garden below with a rope ladder hanging from a treehouse balanced on its branches. My older brothers claimed dominion over the treehouse and deterred any efforts on my part to visit, saying it was too dangerous for girls to climb a rope ladder swinging precipitously over a rock garden. One day I did dare to climb up the rope ladder but my courage failed me when I needed to step off the swinging top rung and onto the floor of the treehouse.

Beyond the copper beech was an orchard filled with a variety of apple trees that I did climb—they were far less daunting than trying to climb into a tree house built on the branches of a large copper beech. A winding flagstone path meandered through the trees under which daffodils and jonquils created an endless yellow carpet in springtime. Anyone exiting the orchard would come across a charming octagonal-shaped summer house with a peaked roof and a bench built around the interior. It was a special place to hide, read a good book, and enjoy the occasional picnic with a playmate or my nanny. South of the formal lawn and separated by a beech hedge was a large kitchen garden that supplied most of our vegetables. Beyond that was a paddock surrounded by a spinney, a wood with thick bushes and narrow path. Sometimes we rented out the paddock to a local farmer and hoped his cattle or horses wouldn't find their way into our vegetable garden.

There were other garden areas: a greenhouse that smelled of dirt and luscious tomatoes, started near the east end of the house and was attached to a brick wall, which also supported the spreading branches of peach trees. On the other side of the wall was the back yard and a long row of sheds with a large double-wooden door opening onto the road. Here the coal merchant entered to unload our supply of coal. One shed housed the coal-burning furnace that heated the main house and greenhouse; another was used for storage, gardening tools, and potting work. Near the back entrance to the laundry room so that Nanny could observe me, the gardeners had constructed a sand box where I loved to create imaginary castles or mix mud pies. Facing the main garden in front of the peach trees, rose-covered arbors formed arches over a crazy paving path. A lavender hedge bordered one side of a rose garden with small geometrically shaped beds framed by low privet hedges. When our younger gardeners had to join up during World War II, all family members would pitch in and do the weeding. By the time we had worked our way through the long pattern of rose beds, the weeds were growing again where we had started. Between the rose garden and orchard, a smaller lawn featured white and purple lilac trees, their sweet perfume filling the air in springtime. Below the high brick walls, which marked the edges of our property, were herbaceous borders with a colorful variety of flowers perfect for picking and arranging.

I remember my mother walking along with a low, flat basket, cutting the flowers and making spectacular displays around the house. She instilled in me a love of flowers, and in time I learned to make posies with layers of short-stemmed flowers in shallow bowls to serve as centerpieces for Mother's tea parties.

Not long after our move to Kirk Ella, my parents bought me a puppy, a white wire-haired fox terrier with black shading over her ears and eyes named Judy. We already had a cat, a black tabby called Billy with a spot of white under his chin. I am sure Mummy and Daddy thought that the new dog would provide companionship for their daughter whose brothers were older and away at school, but I was terrified of this excitable, yapping, puppy who wanted to jump up and lick my face or be petted all the time. After a while she calmed down and enjoyed chasing various critters in the vast gardens, as well as the cat who knew how to escape up a tree when necessary. Judy became especially frustrated when Billy climbed up the exceedingly prickly Monkey Puzzle tree. Both pets had their spots in front of the study fireplace but were not allowed upstairs. I never became an ardent pet lover, but Judy and Billy were an important part of my childhood.

For the first part of our stay at Kirk Ella House we had a full complement of staff. A cook, parlor maid, and nursemaid (Nanny) lived on-site with two cleaning ladies coming every day to dust, vacuum, and polish. My father employed a full-time chauffeur to maintain our cars and to drive him to his consultation rooms and the hospital. On Fridays, he would arrange for the chauffeur to return to Kirk Ella to take my mother into Hull to shop and meet friends for lunch. There were two gardeners and a gardener's boy to manage the grounds. The chauffeur and the head gardener lived in cottages on land owned by my father across the street from our house.

During these early years, my life was ordered and gentle in the typical mode of an upper-class English family. I slept in the night nursery with my nanny, had meals and playtime in the day nursery with its large sunny window overlooking the gardens that offered a great variety of places to explore. I was always dressed in pretty dresses and usually had a bow tying my shoulder-length wavy blonde hair to one side. For special occasions, such as the annual Children's Fancy Dress Ball held in Hull, Nanny used a hot curling iron to make ringlets. When I was six or seven, Mummy would arrange play dates with girls of my age whose parents she knew. But I was never allowed to wander into the village on my own or mingle with the local children because my parents didn't

want me exposed to working class children who would have spoken with regional accents. This sounds snobbish, but that was all part of the British class system. For a short time, before I went away to boarding school and unknown to my parents or even Nanny, I befriended a boy from the village whom I found exploring our paddock. We would meet in the spinney or field and climb trees together.

Romy with ringlets age five

My mother was a good-looking woman with fine, light brown hair, a good figure, and especially beautiful legs. She was well coordinated and athletic, was a member of the Yorkshire Ladies Lacrosse team, and played a solid game of tennis. She kept a well-run house and enjoyed entertaining her husband's colleagues and her own friends. Much of her time was spent managing the servants, planning the week's meals with Edith the cook, ordering food, or shopping at the butchers or fishmonger. She belonged to a Bridge group and had frequent tea parties. Mummy was artistic, had superb taste, and an excellent sense of design. Daddy enjoyed collecting antiques, but Mummy selected the fabrics, furnishings, and oriental rugs with everything made by the best manufacturers. She also loved clothes, dressed in the latest fashions with handbags, shoes, gloves, and hats all coordinated. She had a special cupboard built in the corner of her bedrooms for her shoes. Although I wasn't close to my mother, I admired her, especially her sense of design and organization—attributes that I inherited.

Without a doubt, she instilled in me a love of clothes and an ability to make beautiful selections with everything coordinated.

In the mode of the day, Mother was quite formal and somewhat distant from her children. I saw her on her daily visits upstairs and in the garden, or when she wanted to present me to her friends. Although

Nanny with Billy the cat

she nursed her other babies, Mummy had not been able to nurse me after I was born. This may have contributed to a lack of bonding. But the formal relationship with her was typical of an upper-class English family—visualize a scene from *Downton Abbey* in which the children are brought down by their nursemaids to visit their parents at tea time in the drawing room, or the occasional time when a parent would visit a child in the nursery. Although we were not aristocrats, our lifestyle was similar to the nobility. Not surprisingly, I grew up closer to my nanny than to my mother, always feeling free to share my feelings and secrets with her. Nanny or Nan—her real name was Amy Mary Gibbon—joined our family as a nanny when my second brother, John, was born. She was from Middleton-in-Teesdale, a small market town in County Durham, and was well brought up but had no special training as a nanny. I am sure she stayed in touch with her parents until they died, but we soon became her family. On her days off she would walk into the village to play Whist, a classic English trick-taking card game, with a group of women who had regular social Whist drives, or take a bus into Hull to do some shopping or go to a movie. She lived with us for most of her life, becoming more housekeeper than nanny after we all left home. After Mummy died, Nan continued to live with my youngest brother Bob until he got married, when she found a home as companion to an elderly lady. In 1975, she died peacefully at the age of 81.

In my early years, Nanny would take me out for regular walks and occasionally would find an excuse to buy sweets at the local shop in the village. When they were home from boarding school my older brothers helped to entertain me and teach me to ride my tricycle. They made a dollhouse for me with a fenestrated front that could be removed for access to the interior. It had two stories with a staircase and furniture for each room. We used pieces of old carpeting for the floors and fabric for bedspreads and curtains. Was this preparation for my later career in interior design?

Where Mummy tended to be distant and strict, my father doted on me and was always gentle. He had been so pleased to have a daughter that he gave his wife a beautiful ring with an oval-shaped emerald surrounded by tiny diamonds, which I eventually inherited. I didn't see much of Daddy because he was at the hospital or his consulting rooms every day and didn't come home until just before dinner time. I learned later that he taught me to read when I was about four and half. I have dim memories of sitting on his lap, smelling his pipe tobacco, and looking at books. Starting at age five, I spent mornings at a small, private preschool. To reach the school, Nanny took me past the village church and up a long hill. I came home for lunch and always had a nap in the early afternoon. In 1939, just before my seventh birthday, this idyllic existence changed forever.

2. THE WAR

"We shall go on to the end . . . we shall never Surrender."
—Winston Churchill

On September 3, 1939, a booming voice over a crackling radio brought news into our home and all of Great Britain that, following Adolf Hitler's invasion of Poland, France and Britain had declared war on Germany. Europe had been unstable since the First World War (1914–18), culminating in Hitler and his National Socialist (Nazi) Party re-arming his country and signing treaties with Italy and Japan to satisfy his dream of world domination. The new war would become the biggest and deadliest war in history involving over 30 countries, and lasting six years with an unprecedented loss of life, both in the fighting itself and in the indescribable horror of the Nazi concentration camps, annihilating millions of Jews and fulfilling Hitler's aim to create a master race of pure Aryans.

During our current 21st century Coronavirus pandemic, we listen in horror to daily reports of numbers, in hundreds and thousands, dying from a vicious virus. Statistics are documented by city, county, nation, and globally, sometimes giving the impression that we are competing with other countries to record the largest number of dead. We are reminded of the 1918 Spanish influenza epidemic and, 30 some years later, the second World War reports counting the military, naval, and civilian fatalities.

Along with the rest of Britain my peaceful childhood would never be the same. Hull became one of the most severely damaged British cities with 95 percent of houses destroyed or needing repair. As a port city with water works, gas works, a power station, an oil refinery, six docks, and an important rail terminus, it was especially vulnerable. Moreover, its location was on the route home for the German Luftwaffe, providing a convenient opportunity to unload leftover bombs as the planes followed the river Hull to the Humber estuary and back to their own bases. Half of the city center was destroyed along with many churches, pubs, schools, cinemas, and hospitals. Between 1940 and 1945, the city recorded more than 1,000 hours under alert with 1,200 people killed by the bombing.

Although we lived outside Hull, in the peaceful village of Kirk Ella, we were still affected by the air raids. Homeowners built air raid shelters in their gardens or walked to the nearest communal shelter. We converted a wine cellar under the kitchen into a shelter and had an emergency egress built from the cellar to the outside with the exit stairs shielded by sandbags in case our house was bombed and collapsed on top of us. The entrance to the cellar was from one of the storage rooms off the kitchen. There was a large trap door in the floor with a heavy ring to pull it up. A steep ladder led into the cellar where cubby holes that normally stored wine were converted into sleeping alcoves. In spite of spending many nights in the cellar and trying to sleep on a lumpy mattress in one of the alcoves, I always forgot that I couldn't sit up without bumping my head on the ledge above. In addition to wine, we stored eggs produced by our own chickens. They were kept in a wire basket inside a bucket of Water Glass, a bacteria-resistant solution of sodium silicate that has been around for centuries. It kept the eggs fresh enough for cooking but not very tasty for boiling or frying.

Every evening at dusk my parents and our staff went around the house, closing all the windows, and pulling out heavy wooden shutters that folded into recesses on either side of the window. We also made sure that no light could penetrate to the outside. Accompanying this enforced blackout, our white stucco house had been camouflaged by painting over the white with a pattern of drab colors to prevent it from being a target for German bombers. Every evening at 6:00 P.M. my father turned on the radio to listen to the latest news. He kept a map on the study wall and traced the progress of the armies fighting across Europe with colored push pins.

Having experienced the horrors of the first World War just over 20 years earlier, my parents knew too well what such a conflict entailed. German submarines were already blocking the flow of food, arms, and raw materials to our island. Farmers were struggling to obtain fuel for their machinery and harvest their crops. Clothing manufacturers were forced to make uniforms for the forces or produce fabric for parachutes. Other industrial firms had to produce weapons and equipment for the military and air force. Aircraft production became paramount. Winston Churchill, who succeeded Neville Chamberlain as prime minister on May 10, 1940, was aware that the Royal Air Force had a serious shortage of planes, both fighters and bombers, and lagged far behind the German Luftwaffe. In anticipation of a possible poison gas attack, the government issued 35 million gas masks to civilians who were ordered to carry them at all times. The authorities soon enforced rationing including tea—a vital British staple—at first to two ounces a week, later revised to three ounces a week. Similar to our present predicament, toilet paper was in short supply, forcing King George VI to order some for his family from America. With forethought, my mother had wisely stocked up on many non-perishable essentials, making use of cabinets built in above doors and other storage areas throughout the house.

Although our village was spared the bombing that destroyed so much of Hull, a stray rocket did land at the bottom of our garden, causing the only windows whose wooden shutters had not been closed to explode. We soon adapted to the new routine of nightly air raid sirens. After pulling on our siren suits, a one-piece garment designed by Churchill (his was a sky-blue color) as an easy garment to put on over pajamas for going to air raid shelters, we would hasten downstairs to our wine cellar shelter. Many times, to my mother's dismay, my father would don a metal helmet, commonly known as a "tin hat," and march around the house outside to make sure no lights were visible and to watch the searchlights scanning the sky. We also became accustomed to hearing the sound of planes approaching and learning the difference in resonance between the Royal Air Force and the Luftwaffe.

Peter Wyllie, my future husband, was nine when the war broke out. He was the eldest of three children born to George and

Beatrice Wyllie. Before getting married, George Wyllie had worked for Shell Oil Company as a camp boss in Venezuela and then joined their office staff on his return to England. Soon after the outbreak of war he was called to serve in the army. He was all packed and ready to go when he received a notice that instead of fighting on the front, he could serve his country better by working as a cipher clerk where he would keep track of Shell's ships from their London offices. As the nation's capital and the largest city in Great Britain, London was a prime target for the Luftwaffe. Starting in 1939, in anticipation of a large bombardment, many businesses, banks, radio stations, art collections, and government functions were moved out of the city. Shell's offices were moved to its country club, The Lensbury, on the banks of the Thames near Teddington. Now that George would be working there, the Wyllie family moved from Barkingside in the greater London area to an apartment near Teddington.

Additionally, the Ministry of Health ordered thousands of children accompanied by a few caretakers to be evacuated from London to the countryside. The program, which had three phases linked to different periods of the war—September 1939, when war was declared; June 1940, after the Germans had taken over most of France; and June 1944, when the Germans started attacking with V1 and V2 rockets—displaced more than 3.5 million people. Children, with labels around their necks like pieces of luggage, were packed into trains to go to unknown destinations. Operation Pied Piper was designed by Sir John Anderson who had little comprehension of the emotional turmoil his idea was about to cause. Pete and his younger brother Bruce were among those children. They were sent to stay at the historic town of Ipswich, not far from the North Sea in Suffolk, with an old man who was not happy to house two active boys.

Some children were sent to other parts of the British Empire until September 1940 when an evacuee ship, the City of Benares, was torpedoed by a German submarine causing the loss of 77 displaced children. Following this tragedy, the government decided to put an end to overseas evacuations. All the separations, whether within Britain or abroad, were a terrible hardship both for the parents and the children. Not only did children suffer from family break-ups; some were physically and mentally abused by the strangers who were assigned to take care of them. Supposedly the children who were sent to the countryside were kept safe from bombing raids, but for some the estrangement caused permanent long-term trauma. Even the selection of children by foster families left scars: some were unwanted because they were too young or not strong enough for farm work; others ended up with families who were indifferent to their welfare. Although the war ended in September 1945, the evacuation did not officially end until March 1946 when the authorities were sure that there was no longer any threat of invasion. Post-war studies have shown that children who stayed in their homes and endured the bombing did better psychologically than many of the children who were evacuated.

To raise the spirits of the British people—especially the children—Buckingham Palace arranged for Princess Elizabeth, aged 14, and her sister, Princess Margaret, aged 10, to speak on the BBC's radio broadcast of the Children's Hour: "Thousands of you in this country have had to leave your homes and be separated from your fathers and mothers. My sister Margaret Rose and I feel so much for you as we know from experience what it means to be away from those we love most of all . . . We know every one of us, that in the end all will be well; for God will care for us and give us victory and peace. And when peace comes, remember it will be for us, the children of today, to make the world of tomorrow a better and happier place."

Eighty years later the whole world is at war, not with a human enemy but with a virus for which mankind has no immunity. As thousands die and people are forced to hunker down at home to avoid becoming infected with COVID-19, the Queen, now aged 93, has once again spoken to her subjects: "While we have faced challenges before, this one is different . . . This time we join with all nations across the globe in a common endeavor, using the great advances of science and our instinctive compassion to heal. We will succeed—and that success will belong to every one of us. We should take comfort that while we may have more still to endure, better days will return: we will be with our friends again; we will be with our families again; we will meet again." The Queen mentioned that the painful sense of separation from their loved ones caused by social distancing reminded her of World War II. Although children are not being evacuated, they are forced to stay home from school and college, taking unsatisfactory virtual classes, missing graduations, and most of all missing contact with friends and teachers.

Because there was no bombing in 1939, many parents, including the Wyllies, brought their children back to the city. However,

Germany had already taken over much of Europe, including the Netherlands, Belgium, and Northern France. In late May 1940, with little hope of stopping the German advance, Churchill made the decision to evacuate the British and Allied Forces from France. The Dunkirk evacuation, which rescued 338,000 men from May 26 to June 4, soon became a memorable episode. After the French capitulated, there was genuine fear that the Nazis would invade England. They now had bases both in France and the low countries (Belgium and the Netherlands) putting them closer to England's south and north coasts. The British government gave the anticipated invasion the code name "Cromwell." All church bells were silenced so that they could be rung to warn people if an invasion had started. In preparation for an invasion, Hitler order the Luftwaffe, aided by their advanced navigational beams, to weaken the RAF by targeting their air bases and destroying as many of their planes as possible. But the planned invasion had to be delayed because of bad weather.

Although Hitler and Churchill had a temporary agreement not to bomb each other's capitals, a German plane inadvertently dropped its bombs on London, enabling Churchill to order the bombing of Berlin. In retaliation, from September 1940 to May 1941, the Germans began bombing London, making the most of moonlit nights and using incendiary bombs to start fires and light the way for the heavy bombers. Known as the Blitz, the nightly raids caused enormous devastation to the capital with tens of thousands of buildings destroyed, nearly 30,000 Londoners killed, and hundreds of thousands of people made homeless. As buildings collapsed, centuries-old dust created dense fogs, reduced visibility, caused many of those newly homeless to choke, and made it especially difficult for medical personnel to clean wounds.

Boosted by Churchill's magnificent oratory to endure the onslaught, people tried to keep working, but inevitably the nightly bombing affected morale, especially as winter brought longer and darker nights. Many Londoners suffered from a lack of sleep because of the constant noise: wailing sirens, the thunder of heavy bombers filling the sky, the relentless crack of anti-aircraft guns, the whistling of falling bombs, and the reverberating explosions of buildings crashing to the ground. With everything blacked out, injuries were more frequent as citizens drove or walked into obstacles. In addition to buildings, both famous and mundane, factories and warehouses were destroyed, leaving an even greater shortage of everyday commodities, such as sugar, coffee, tea, cheese, bacon, ham, jams, and marmalade.

Although underground stations were designated shelters, many citizens feared being trapped underground and preferred above-ground metal shelters, named for Sir John Anderson, the Home Secretary who devised the evacuation plans. The arched shelters were made of galvanized corrugated steel panels, sometimes built into a hillside with earth and grass coverings. Pete's family, who lived in an apartment house, shared an Anderson shelter with other residents. It had been built at the bottom of a large common garden below a railroad embankment. At first when the sirens sounded, the Wyllie family dutifully took refuge in the shelter. However, they soon tired of the constant traipsing in night clothes to a cold and dank place. Leaving their sons to sleep through the night alarms, Pete's parents stayed up, kept watch, and hoped that nothing serious would happen.

Some children adapt well to their circumstances, and boys especially are good at making the most of wartime conditions. Pete bicycled to Hampton Grammar School, enjoying the opportunity to compete with his friends in searching for the greatest number and largest piece of shrapnel, discarded by shells or exploded bombs during the previous night's raids.

During the latter part of the war, 1944–45, Germany developed pilotless V1 and V2 rockets, known as buzz bombs. The V1s were flying bombs fired from Northern France, now occupied by the Germans, and the V2 rockets were launched from the Netherlands. Both were aimed at London, killing over a thousand civilians and injuring many more. As they flew overhead the V1s pulse jet engine made a whining noise followed by silence before landing and exploding; the V2s came without any warning sound. Pete remembers cycling home and hearing a V1 flying above him and heading toward his home. Fortunately for him, it hit a nearby shopping area instead of his house. As he cycled frantically along, Pete saw a shop's large plate glass window vibrate from the explosion before the glass shattered and fell to the ground.

In June 1940, people were evacuated from some of the south coast communities and my parents worried that Hull's position on the Humber estuary facing the North Sea made it especially open to infiltration. Cognizant of these dangers, and following the recommendations of the Ministry of Health, my father decided that mother and I should evacuate to the Lake District. My brothers, who were already away at boarding school, were relatively safe. It was a difficult decision and an emotional time. My father, of course, had to stay to fulfill his medical duties and help the many wounded civilians. I recall seeing my mother crying at dinner shortly before we left. Along with some other evacuees from our community we stayed for several months in the small hamlet of Borrowdale in Cumbria, where the River Derwent drains into Derwentwater. About 175 miles from Hull, it was quiet and well away from the bombing or possible invasion, but it was an anxious time for everyone. Mummy had friends to play Bridge with but I missed my nanny and I didn't like the food and became very thin. I did, however, have other young girls about my age to play with and explore the local streams and hotel grounds. One day after sitting down on a rock, I discovered to my horror that I had sat on an ant nest. I ran screaming to the hotel disrupting my mother's Bridge game with the news that I was covered in ants. Mother rushed me upstairs, stripped off all my clothes, and immersed me in the bath tub. Afterward I was much more careful where I walked or sat.

During our enforced evacuation, Mummy didn't feel quite right. She was in her early 40s and wondered if she had started her menopause. To her shock and surprise a visit to a doctor confirmed that she was pregnant. What a time to get pregnant! Not only was she concerned about her age, but even more about bringing a baby into the world in the middle of a war. When she told her husband, he was in disbelief in spite of being responsible, and when he shared the news with his medical colleagues, they teased him.

After staying until the end of summer, Mummy and I returned from the Lake District to Hull. In spite of the threat of air raids, Mummy was anxious to get home, be with her husband, see her sons, and visit her own gynecologist. There would be significant changes to both our lives in the year ahead.

BOARDING SCHOOL

3. QUEEN MARY'S SCHOOL

Queen Mary's School is a girls' preparatory boarding school originally housed in the mansion of Duncombe Park, near Helmsley, Yorkshire.

September 1940: Following the Blitz of London, many major cities became targets for bombing. These included important port towns such as Hull, Portsmouth, Plymouth, and Southampton, and the industrial cities of Birmingham, Manchester, Liverpool, and Coventry, the latter of which suffered an intense all-night attack. So many people were killed that mass funerals were necessary. Among the buildings destroyed was Coventry's famous 14th Century Gothic Cathedral, whose ruins now form a garden of remembrance next to a starkly modern church.

After returning from Borrowdale in September 1940 and being confronted with daily news of the horrendous destruction occurring across the country, my parents decided I would be safer tucked away in the countryside at an elite preparatory boarding school. In England at the time, it was customary for upper-class families to send their children to boarding schools. My brothers were already at Fettes College, an Edinburgh boarding school

Duncombe Park's Father Time with the Ionic Temple in the background

43

for boys focused on sports and tough training, such as cold showers in the morning. In normal times my parents would have waited another year before sending me away from home, but these were not normal times. I was seven years old and would turn eight in November 1940, when I was enrolled at Queen Mary's School.

Nathaniel Woodard, a Church of England priest, founded the Woodard Corporation (formerly the Society of St. Nicholas) for the purpose of establishing a group of primary and secondary schools to educate boys and girls in the values of the Anglican church. The flagship school was Lancing College founded in 1848. Other schools followed, and in 1925 the Corporation established a girls' prep school in the mansion of Duncombe Park, near Helmsley, Yorkshire. With a rapid increase in enrollment by 1931, the School of Duncombe Park was renamed Queen Mary's School. Eventually it became the preparatory school for two senior schools, Queen Ethelburga's and Queen Margaret's. For most of her childhood my mother and her sisters were tutored at home, but in her last two years mother attended Queen Margaret's School. I would eventually move on to Queen Ethelburga's School in Harrogate.

Duncombe Park is owned by the Duncombe family whose leading members acquired the title of Earl and Countess Feversham. The head of the family is now Jasper Orlando Slingsby Duncombe, 7th Baron Feversham, born in 1968. The Fevershams leased their estate to Queen Mary's School for 60 years until 1986. The school then moved to Baldersby Park, near Thirsk in North Yorkshire, and the estate was returned to the family. Although the house now belongs to Jake Duncombe, a younger son of the sixth Baron Feversham, the gardens and parkland are open to the public, and the gardens are considered some of the finest in England.

The Italianate baroque house that became the opulent home for our 75-member, elite boarding school has an interesting history. The house was designed in 1711 by English architect William Wakefield. In 1843 Sir Charles Barry constructed additions. Sixteen years after a fire in 1879 gutted the interior, William Young rebuilt the house using the original design with some necessary modifications to the interior.

For us school children, the house was a magical place with stories of ghosts, secret passageways, woodwork that oozed blood, and turrets around which the wind howled at night. The first-floor rooms became the school's dining room, main assembly hall, library, music room, offices, classrooms, and chapel. Family portraits in ornate gilded frames remained hanging in the main reception rooms. In the dining room I remember one grand lady in particular, who had eyes that seemed to peer into your inner being and follow you wherever you sat. On the second floor, spacious bedrooms were divided into cubicles with curtains that could be drawn for privacy. Each room had senior children helping to look after the youngsters. My first year was memorable for a painful accident when a strong wind caused a heavy door to close on my finger. The middle finger nail on my right hand eventually came off and has never been the same since. I also got into trouble for sharing my specially prescribed Calcium vitamins with some of the other girls. Matron reported the incident to the Head Mistress who gave me a severe reprimand and smacked my hand with a ruler.

The school's Head Mistress Miss Bowen, and her sec-ond-in-command Miss Brown, were stern but well-meaning spinsters from New Zealand. They managed a devoted staff of teachers and ran a tight ship during the challenging wartime years. When one of my mother's friends asked if I was homesick, I said no because I thought she meant was I throwing up. I didn't know what homesick meant, but I am sure I missed my nanny. She would have told me where to put my dirty handkerchiefs. Instead, I stuffed them under the mattress only to be discovered when it was time to go home for the holidays. Gladys, a house-keeper who did all the mending and helped Matron at bath time and reminded me of my nanny, was especially kind to me proba-bly because I was younger than most of the children. She had cats in her basement workroom and gave me the nickname "Pussy." When we took our weekly baths, I remember her gently scrub-bing my back and washing my light brown hair. She also taught me how to darn, a skill that proved useful many years later when I was dating my future husband at the University of St. Andrews.

The school curriculum covered the important elementary subjects: Reading, Writing and Arithmetic, as well as History and Botany, and in the senior years we began Latin and French. Daily gym, dancing, and outdoor games kept us fit, and instruc-tion in needlework, music, and religion put the finishing touches to our education. We learned carols and hoped to be selected for a role in the traditional Christmas pageant. In addition to our daily classes in the setting of this elegant house, we had 30 acres of enthralling grounds and formal gardens to explore. The garden façade of the house itself, with its pedimented and columned center, had full-height arched windows punctuating the ground

Queen Mary's gym students performing in front of Duncombe Park house

floor and opening onto an extensive terrace. Steps led to a broad green lawn surrounded by curving flower beds. At the far end of the lawn was a statue of Father Time leaning over a sundial designed by British sculptor John van Nost. Adjacent lawns, with grass edges sloping down to gravel pathways, served as outdoor stages for our dance and theatrical performances. Farther away from the main house were wooded walks that led to long terraces. A walk through a dense and dark arbor of bowed ewe trees led to one of two temples positioned at each end of a green terrace, with surprise views of the River Rye and the village of Helmsley. Both temples were designed by John Vanbrugh, the architect who created Blenheim Palace and Castle Howard. One temple is in the Greek Doric style with a closed interior and columns supporting a dome. The other temple is more like a garden gaze-bo with columns terminating in Ionic-style capitals and an open interior. Both were enchanting places to visit while we searched for wildflowers. The picked flowers were placed in glass jars with names written on lined paper alongside each jar. Our task was to learn their names and complete a test. I was especially fond of bluebells.

Occasionally we took field trips away from the gardens of the main house into the estate's vast parkland. In earlier times the open space was a deer park for Helmsley Castle with areas for raising different types of deer. The estate sold venison until World War II when all the deer were butchered and the park became an army training camp. After the army moved in with their tanks, armored vehicles, and shooting ranges, we were forbidden to visit. Our parents had sent us to the country to be free of the trappings of war and then suddenly the war and its preparations was on our doorstep. One early morning we were woken by a huge explosion. A convoy of tanks rolling down the road created so much vibration that a clock tower, which stood guard on one side of the house's entrance, collapsed. The accident occurred only a few minutes before a maintenance man was due to climb the tower to wind the clock. It was a traumatic event and a strong reminder of the army's presence. For many years I kept a small piece of stucco from the collapsed tower.

Another example of the war's proximity was an encampment for Italian prisoners of war. My music teacher, Miss Faddi, was Italian and used to visit the prisoners to cheer them up. Of course, we imagined that she was plotting their escape, but no such event happened. For some reason my music instruction started with the violin. I can remember the abysmal rasping noise created by my bow wavering across the strings. Miss Faddi, who sympathized with my efforts but realized that I had no natural talent for music, suggested piano lessons, which I dutifully took for the rest of my boarding school years.

A traditional school outing was an Ascension Day trip to Rievaulx Abbey, about four miles from Helmsley. Founded in 1132, Rievaulx was the first Cistercian abbey inaugurated in the north of England. Until 1538 when Henry VIII dissolved all the monasteries, it was one of the most influential and spiritually prominent centers of monasticism in Britain. The spectacular ruins provided a fascinating playground for us children to explore. Our teachers also made sure we studied the original plans and the history of the abbey. We tried to imagine the monks going about their daily activities, eating, reading, and praying in the now roofless spaces surrounded by walls interspersed with arched openings and passageways that led to underground tunnels. After an energetic morning of discovery, we would enjoy a picnic lunch and, occasionally, a special treat of ice cream—a rarity during the wartime years.

Once or twice a term we had a special weekend when our parents came to visit. Most of them stayed in the only hotel in the picturesque market town of Helmsley. Congenially referred to as the Mucky Duck, the Black Swan is a 500-year-old inn made up of three sections from different historic periods: Elizabethan, Tudor, and Georgian. In 1838, it became one of the stops for the Helmsley Highflyer, a stage coach that allowed travelers to journey between Helmsley, Leeds, and York. My parent's visits to Helmsley gave them a chance to see their daughter in her school setting and provided a respite from the travails of the war. I enjoyed showing off my achievements in school and being able to savor high tea at the Mucky Duck. During the war special sandwiches and cakes were extravagant treats. Sweets (candies) were rationed but our parents were allowed to send us care packages, as long as we shared the contents with other children.

At the end of each year, Queen Mary's held a special parents' day, with appropriate dance and play performances set among the beautiful gardens that provided a perfect backdrop for costumed actors, including one mounted on a horse. The grand terrace and steps in front of the main garden façade formed a stage for speeches and prize giving. In deference to wartime shortages and the needs of people affected by the bombing, prizes consisted of a simple certificate in place of a book. The certificate stated that: "Rosemary Blair was this Year (1942) entitled to a Prize for Good Work through the year, Form IIIB, and gave it for the Relief of Distress." This unusual terminology indicated that instead of buying a book, the money was given to an organization that helped citizens and soldiers who were suffering war-related injuries or psychological distress. Wearing my blue uniform dress and my short hair clipped to one side, I walked up the steps to receive my certificate from Miss Bowen and a guest of honor who had been invited to give away the prizes.

Typical of most boarding schools and colleges, the year was divided into three terms. In between terms we went back to our families for several weeks with summer the longest vacation. Although the Battle of Britain began in August 1940, the dreaded invasion never happened. Bad weather, expected to escalate during the winter months, kept thwarting Hitler's efforts. His Luftwaffe encountered greater resistance than expected from the RAF, especially their fighter planes, Spitfires, and Hurricanes. The Fuhrer also had an unrealistic expectation that Churchill would surrender. Following the intense bombing of 1940 and 1941, Hitler became concerned about two things: the Americans would increase their aid to Britain or even enter the war; and the Russians were sounding ominously threatening, forcing Hitler to declare war on them, diverting both his attention and his armies.

Every time I returned home, I was shocked by the destruction in Hull; it seemed as though on every corner there was a pile of rubble. Born on March 16, 1941, during the worst of the bombing, my baby brother Bob was affected in strange ways. He would lull himself to sleep at night by humming and turning his head from side to side as though he was mimicking the sounds of sirens or planes flying overhead. He also created bombed out scenes by building a heap of toys and bricks in the corner of the nursery. When Bob was a few months old, he and his cot were moved into the night nursery to sleep with Nanny, and I was moved into a bedroom of my own. My new room was the former guest bedroom. It was quite large with twin beds, two tall windows, a fireplace, wash basin, a built-in closet, and a large free-standing wardrobe. Perhaps, because I now slept alone, I found the room scary, imagining as I went to sleep that there might be a monster in the antique wardrobe. My siren suit always lay at the foot of the bed, ready to be pulled on over my pajamas when I heard the wailing of the sirens, and knew that we had to rush down the stairs to our wine cellar shelter.

Occasionally, during a school holiday my father would take me with him to visit the Crippled Children's School, which had been evacuated to Lincolnshire on the other side of the Humber River. It was a special adventure that required taking the ferry across the river. Although I had no exposure to poor children who grew up on "the other side of the tracks," and lacked limbs at birth because of congenital amputation, limb defect, or malnutrition, I was struck by their cheerfulness as they waited to be examined by Doctor Blair. My father was doing pioneering work by fitting these children with protheses in different sizes to accommodate their growth and help them function.

For an island at war, with many factories dedicated to producing armaments and clothing for the forces, and farms struggling to provide enough food, rationing was essential. One of the biggest challenges for any mother was managing the coupon books not only for food but for clothes. My brothers and I had to wear school uniforms, and it was a struggle to allocate our limited supply of coupons for the bare necessities of school clothes. It would not have been our family's normal practice to wear second-hand clothes, but in these circumstances, Mother was only too happy to obtain used school uniforms. She became adept at meting out our coupons for food and persuading the butcher to provide some decent cuts of meat, and the fishmonger to let her know when there had been a good catch. Food was scarcer in London, and Pete admits that one year his parents were desperate enough to kill his pet rabbits for stew.

Although our current COVID-19 stay at home and social distancing regulations do not include rationing, it might help stave off the unreasonable hoarding of cleaning supplies, hand sanitizer, and paper goods. More serious is the shortage of protective clothing, equipment, and ventilators for the medical community, putting our doctors and nurses at serious risk of contracting the virus.

During our present scourge, most states require their citizens to wear face masks in public. Some people object strongly to this directive; it seems a small price to pay, however, for avoiding infection and a minor inconvenience compared to the gas masks that were issued to British civilians at the start of the war as protection against poison gas bombs that might be dropped by the Luftwaffe. Although it was 20 years since the first World War, memories of chlorine gas and mustard gas being used on troops had left unforgettable memories. My father had been gassed. He survived, but the gas caused health problems for the rest of his life. The government-issued masks were made of rubber, covered your whole face with goggle eye pieces, a big tube-like protrusion in the front, and broad straps holding the mask to your head. We had to carry them with us at all times. They were packed into an ugly, square, cardboard box, making them clumsy to hold against your body with a strap over your shoulder. On many occasions people had to wear them during the severest bombing raids, and we all had to practice putting them on and off at least once a week.

Just as the 2020 pandemic has limited travel both nationally and internationally, vacations during World War II were either out of the question or restricted to places within easy reach of home. Because of his medical work, Daddy could hardly ever leave Hull, but occasionally Mummy would take us to the seaside, usually Scarborough. One of my best friends at Queen Mary's was Gwyneth Snowball. Her mother rented a small cabin on the oceanfront in Scarborough. It wasn't a place to stay, but a one-room, glass-fronted bungalow overlooking the beach, with a small kitchen and bathroom and a place to shelter from the ever-present wind. Gwyneth and I, armed with buckets and nets, would paddle in the tide pools, bringing back our pails filled with tiny shrimp that Mrs. Snowball would cook. We would then sit on the cabin's deck and spend happy hours shelling and eating our tasty catch.

Adjusting to the new rhythm of a country at war, Mummy forsook her usual tea parties and gathered her friends together to knit garments for the soldiers—all in dreary khaki color, a name meaning earth-colored derived from Hindustani. The group created scarves, gloves, balaclavas (face masks), and sweaters. Eager to bring me into the fold, Mummy and her friends taught me to knit, probably just a simple scarf, but it was the beginning of a knitting hobby I still enjoy today. Now, in place of knitted balaclavas, I am sewing face masks to protect my family members and friends from the dreaded microbes of COVID-19 that have invaded our world.

In the 1940s, before the development of immunizations, sickness of various kinds, especially communicable diseases such as measles, mumps, and chicken pox were common in a boarding school. A wing of the main building was made into a Sanatorium where children were sent to be quarantined and nursed back to health. One term I had one of the dreaded diseases—I think it was chicken pox—and was placed in a turret bedroom to keep me away from other children. In addition to being lonely, I was frightened. There were scary sounds: dripping water coming from a water tank in a closet, the howling of the wind around the turret, and the image of ghosts wandering the corridors of the old mansion. One night the wind was so strong that it blew open the large sash window above my bed; hearing my screams, a nurse came to my rescue and closed the window.

I was also prone to earaches and many times had to rest in bed instead of playing games outdoors. During the second year at school I experienced an especially severe earache. Although the doctor was called to examine me, he didn't immediately recognize the severity of my ear infection. Finally, after several days of extreme pain, my parents were called. My doctor father suspected immediately that the infection was serious enough to require surgery. He and my mother drove to Duncombe Park, wrapped me up in a blanket, and lay me in the back of the car, setting off immediately to get back to Hull. It was nighttime, and many villages and highways had had their signposts removed to confuse the enemy in the case of an invasion. I can still remember this terrifying drive with my father, using only slit-eyed headlights, having to negotiate unmarked, narrow country roads and stay clear of a convoy of military tanks and vehicles coming in the opposite direction. We finally arrived at a private nursing home in Hull where an ear, nose, and throat surgeon performed an emergency mastoidectomy, a surgical procedure to remove diseased mastoid air cells in the skull near the inner ear. The procedure was successful and saved my life. After the war this kind of surgery became rare because such infections are now treated with penicillin, discovered by Arthur Fleming in 1928 and further developed by other scientists. During the war the use of penicillin was restricted to the armed forces. With the loving care of the nursing home staff, who coddled the daughter of their most respected doctor, my recovery was slow but steady. After two weeks I was released to my home where I spent the rest of the spring term.

In spite of the bombings in England and the terrible happenings on the continent, the war years at Queen Mary's had their bright moments. One year, King George VI and Queen Elizabeth visited to inspect the troops that were stationed at Duncombe Park, and the students were allowed to gather on the school's front steps to see their arrival. Another time we had the honor of witnessing the beginning of a hunt when the local gentry met in the front courtyard. It was a spectacular sight with the leading huntsmen in their "pink" coats and many of the ladies riding side saddle—all on the finest of horses surrounded by a pack of barking hounds eager to sniff out and chase the fox once the horn had signaled the beginning of the hunt.

In 1945, at the age of 12, I said a sad goodbye to Queen Mary's and with trepidation moved on to my senior school, Queen Ethelburga's.

4. QUEEN ETHELBURGA'S SCHOOL

"To be the best that I can with the gifts that I have."
—QES Hill Standard

Queen Ethelburga's foundation stone with its inscription "Pro deo et ecclesia—For God and the Church" was laid by Viscountess Mountgarret in 1910, and the school was officially opened in September 1912 by the Duchess of Albany. The success of Queen Margaret's in Escrick Park near York, founded in 1901, had proved the need for more good boarding schools in the north of England. This time, as part of Nathaniel Woodard's foundation, the directors decided that the new school should be housed in brand new buildings on a grand scale. An Irish peer, Viscount Mountgarret, provided the site, a loan for the construction, and money for the initial expense. The buildings were strung along a hilltop on the edge of Harrogate, Yorkshire. Four houses served as residences for approximately 160 students, with a main building for classes, assemblies, and offices, and most important of all, a beautiful, free-standing chapel given by Lord Mountgarret and dedicated to St. Aiden. Behind the buildings were the school's tennis courts and playing fields extending to the open moors.

The school was named for Queen Ethelburga, a Christian born in the late sixth century to King Ethelberht of Kent. She became the second wife of Edwin, the Anglo-Saxon king of Northumbria from 626 to 633 CE. As a condition of his marriage, Edwin agreed that he and his Northumbrians would forsake their Paganism and convert to Christianity. The names of the school's residences were Cantwara, Derwent, Eoforwic, and Lyminge—all places associated with the life of King Edwin and Queen Ethelburga. Cantwara and Eoforwic were the Anglo-Saxon names for Canterbury and York respectively.

The school buildings had survived World War I without being commandeered, but when war broke out again in 1939, His Majesty's Office of Works requisitioned Queen Ethelburga's buildings for national purposes. With the stipulation that the information was "Official secret," the school's managers found it difficult to advertise for a temporary location. But with the help of the school's Bursar, Mr. R. F. Pawsey, a temporary home was found. Commander and Lady Doris Vyner offered their mansion, Studley Royal, near Ripon along with some additional buildings and a wing of Fountains Hall near Fountains Abbey. Some of the staff were housed in farms and houses nearby.

When I enrolled at Queen Ethelburga's in September 1945, the school was still in its wartime evacuation home of Studley Royal. The house stood in the north-west corner of the Studley Estate, which included the remains of Fountains Abbey (another 12th century Cistercian monastery), Fountains Hall, St. Mary's Church, and the renowned Studley Royal Water Garden. Created by John Aislabie in 1718, the ornamental lakes, canals, temples, and cascades encompass one of the best surviving examples of a Georgian water garden in England. Describing the school's stay at Studley Royal, headmistress Miss Evelyn Young wrote: "The beauty of the Park with its trees and the deer, the lovely country walks and Fountains [Abbey] and its grounds were all uplifting and the peace of our surroundings gave comfort and courage in a world of raids and bombs."

Following a fire in 1716, John Aislabie rebuilt the original medieval manor house of Studley Royal and constructed a main block between the former projecting wings. His son William added a portico in 1762, completing the mansion's Palladian style. The school children and staff enjoyed the village and took walks in the vast estate. I remember walking through the estate to St. Mary's Church, experiencing a sense of wonder among the many trees and flowering bushes, and being fascinated by the ruins and history of Fountains Abbey. The house itself had many large reception rooms and bedrooms that the school divided into cubicles. A beautiful, double staircase became a dramatic setting for Nativity plays: the stable with Mary, Joseph, and baby was positioned on the central mezzanine, angels and kings stood on the two arms of the stairs leading from the landing above, shepherds gathered on the central flight leading down from the mezzanine, and the audience was arranged in the hall below.

As with other historic buildings and the families who owned them, rumors abounded. One was a mythical story that the many tragedies suffered by the Vyner family were the result of a curse placed on them after a stolen jewel was hidden in the foundations of Fountains Hall. Already in its long history the house had been destroyed by fire, and in 1946 during the Easter holidays, just as the school was moving back to Harrogate, another terrible fire raged through the house, destroying everything in its path. To my shock, I learned that the fire had started when a beam caught alight in the chimney of a fireplace in the bedroom where I had been sleeping. The Vyners lost valuable pictures and furniture, and the school many of its possessions, including a portrait of Miss Evelyn Young, the founding headmistress, all the contents of the acting cupboard, and eighteen pianos.

Winston Churchill had been striving in vain for two years to persuade President Franklin Roosevelt to overcome his country's opposition to participate in another world war. Finally, in January 1941, the United States Government passed a Lend-Lease Bill, allowing them to lend, rather than sell, much needed ships, supplies, and food to Great Britain and its allies. Nevertheless, the US remained officially neutral until their navy was attacked by the Japanese at Pearl Harbor on December 8, 1941. This tragic event was the trigger that compelled America to enter the war. It still took more than two years of conflict on many fronts in Europe, the Middle East, and the Pacific before D-Day when, on June 6, 1944, the Allied forces invaded Normandy and forced the Germans to retreat. War ended in Europe when a peace treaty was signed on May 8, 1945, with Winston Churchill announcing VE Day. Germany had surrendered about a week after Adolf Hitler committed suicide, finally bringing an end to the devastating conflict and the unspeakable shock of the concentration camps. Everyone rejoiced with street parties— people shouting, singing, and dancing—all over Britain. I was at home and celebrated with my brothers and parents. We raised the Union Jack on our flagpole and broke open a bottle of champagne. Sadly, it took two atomic bombs dropped on Hiroshima and Nagasaki in August 1945 to coerce the Japanese to capitulate. The formal surrender took place on September 2,

1945, aboard the battleship U.S.S. *Missouri* in Tokyo Bay, and became known as V-J Day.

Meanwhile in Harrogate, the army moved out of the school's hilltop buildings. Following some necessary cleaning and repainting, the children and staff were able to return home. After six years there were no girls left who knew the original buildings, but with the help of Miss Young, eight of her staff, and two Old Ethelburgians, they acclimated to the new setting.

School days followed a rigid routine with many rules governing our behavior. At times it seemed oppressive, and we were frequently tempted to talk when we were supposed to be silent, or run when we should be walking, or be untidy when we should have been neat. Looking back on my school years, I realize how much the discipline, sense of organization, and training contributed to my ability to cope with the challenges that life brought my way. While at Queen Ethelburga's, I was a member of Eoforwic house. Each student had her own cubicle with partial height partitions and a curtain across the doorway. The cubicles were furnished with a single bed, wardrobe, dresser, and chair. We were permitted to have our own eiderdowns to keep us warm, and a few photographs and ornaments to decorate our dressers. Every morning, after a strip-wash in tepid water, we dressed and made our beds. We were taught to make our beds army fashion with the sheets so tightly tucked in that you could bounce a penny on the top. Corners of the sheets and blanket had to be folded like an envelope and the eiderdown carefully rolled back at the end of the bed. We were taught how to fold our clothes and store them neatly in the dresser drawers, with our tunics and overalls and a few clothes from home hung in the wardrobe. Every day the house matron inspected our cubicles, and our tidiness or lack thereof was graded. At the end of each term those with perfect scores received a gold star that was attached to the frame of our cubicle doorway. By the time I graduated from Queen Ethelburga's I had received more gold stars than any other student. I still fold my clothes and feel that it isn't right to start the day without making my bed.

Our uniforms were elaborate and compulsory. Because of its location on the top of a hill, the school was often extremely cold in winter, especially when the wind blew off the moors and propelled its way along the covered walkway linking the buildings. Between our vests (undershirts) and long-sleeved blouses, we wore liberty bodices. This was a garment for women and girls that had been developed at the end of the 19th century in place of a corset. On top of our underwear and stockings held up by suspenders we wore a brown, pleated tunic held at the waist with a brown girdle or, in the case of those girls who had passed the good deportment test, a golden girdle. I had a golden girdle. To keep everything clean during classes, this assemblage of garments was topped by a blue overall with pockets. For walking from our houses to the main school building or to the chapel, we wore brown cloaks with hoods to give us some protection from the everpresent, vicious wind. For gym, we stripped down to our blouses and special gym bloomers, and for outdoor sports, we wore our tunics without the overalls. In summer, we discarded the liberty bodices, wore lighter-weight blouses and straw hats for special outings. Senior girls were permitted to walk into Harrogate to look around the shops, have tea, or even attend a suitable movie. However, school hats were a must for such outings. One time my friends and I

Queen Ethelburga's – Romy in her school uniform

removed our hats. We were trying to hide our school appearance and blend with the general populace. Not surprisingly, someone reported us to the school authorities. To our embarrassment, our punishment was to wear hats all day in school for the next two weeks.

After breakfast we would gather in the Assembly Hall in the main school building for morning prayers and announcements. The rest of the morning was spent in our classrooms according to our grade where we had assigned desks and received instruction in all academic subjects: English, History, Mathematics, Geography, French, and Latin. We also had science classes taught in a laboratory where we learned the basics of biology, including cutting up and dissecting frogs and other small creatures; I can distinctly remember the smell of the formaldehyde in which the frogs were kept. Art, Music, and Divinity rounded out our education. Daily gymnastics in a well-equipped gymnasium was compulsory. Unless the weather was too wet and bleak, we played field sports outside every day. Fortunately, I was well-coordinated and enjoyed all the physical exercise. I began learning tennis when I was 12, first on grass courts and then on clay when I was good enough to be on a team. Three of us who were best friends, were team members: Shirley Wray was Captain of the 1st VI; Frances Coward and I were partners and I was Captain of the 2nd VI. Miss Evelyn Young would often stand on the side of the court and admonish or urge us on during matches, reminding us that we were playing for the team and the school, not for ourselves. I also played lacrosse and cricket, and in my senior years, was a member of these teams, and captain of the gym team. We enjoyed inter-house contests and played matches against other schools

Romy as Captain of QES gym team

like Queen Margaret's and Harrogate Ladies' College. One of our physical education teachers, who was a member of the English Women's cricket team, gave us excellent coaching and inspired us by her example. My grandfather was an ardent follower of cricket, and occasionally I would attend the test matches with him when they were held in Scarborough, not far from home. I found that the best way to focus on the three-day events was to keep score, which also helped me learn the intricacies of the game.

A gym teacher, on whom I had a crush, was our Girl Guide leader. She had naturally wavy hair and big brown eyes. As part of our training, we went away on camping trips and learned how to erect center pole bell tents, how to mix porridge, and how to cook bacon and eggs for breakfast or beans on toast for supper. Much of the time it rained, and we had to keep swinging the tents so that the entrances were not always a path of mud. We slept in sleeping bags on lumpy mattresses made by filling bags with straw. The experience left me with a distinct dislike for camping. However, after I married, I managed an extensive camping trip across America, and when we had children, I agreed that it would be good for them to experience sleeping outdoors under canvas.

In 1934, one of the temporary buildings that housed some of the early students and the first school dog, was converted into a swimming pool. During the war, the pool stood empty but was filled and put back into action a year or two after our return to Harrogate. Finally, we had a chance to learn swimming. But for those of us who were older (I was 14) swimming didn't come easily. I was scared of the water and especially of the deep end. One day I finally plucked up courage to swim a length of the pool making sure to stay near the edge in case I faltered. Just as I was crossing the deepest part, I had to push away from the wall to avoid another student. I panicked, lost confidence, and went under, came to the surface and went under again. Finally, a staff member saw what was happening, dove in and rescued me. I have never forgotten the feeling of being submerged, fighting for air, and feeling that I was sinking fast to the bottom never to come up again. The experience left me with a permanent fear of deep water. Eventually, I learned to do the breast stroke with my face in the water, and I use our California swimming pool on a regular basis during the summer.

Every day ended with a service in the chapel. In the evenings we were allowed to change out of our uniforms into "home" clothes and enjoy hobbies, puzzles, games, and each other's company in the common rooms of our houses. Four of us in Eoforwic became best friends: Frances Coward, Eileen Lees, Shirley Wray, and I. Like most school children, we gave each other silly nicknames: Frances was "Cow," Eileen was "Fleas," Shirley was "Wray," and I was "Blair." After leaving school, we stayed in touch but have only seen each other on rare occasions.

Silence was the golden rule at night, when we got up in the morning, during classes and school gatherings, and of course in chapel. The chapel, a lovely, simple, Gothic-inspired structure, was the heart of the school. In addition to daily evening prayers, two services were held on a Sunday, a morning communion and evensong. Music was an important element of the school with many pupils taking private lessons in piano and other instruments (I continued my piano lessons), music appreciation, and choir under the direction of Miss Reeks. My best friend, Frances, was in the choir. I longed to be a member, but my inability to sing in tune prevented me from passing the test. Although I was never part of the choir, I did manage to achieve a position in the choir loft as an organ pumper. Like many small churches, the school had a pump organ, a type of organ that generates sound as air flows past a vibrating piece of thin metal or reed. The volume and tonal range were more limited than an electronic organ but the instrument was cheaper and took up less space. To help the player play, it was necessary to pump air into the organ with a long lever on one side. All went well unless the "pumper" became distracted or fell asleep and the organ ran out of air. To my dismay I let this happen, but only one time. Afterward I was careful never to spark the anger of Miss Reeks again.

The chapel was also the location for our confirmations—mine on November 26, 1947, by the Bishop of Ripon—followed by our first communion. As a senior girl I took my turn in reading a lesson at the Sunday morning service. I also served at the Communion service and learned to swing the Thurible, a brass censer with chains that held the burning incense and was an important part of the traditional ceremony of the Anglican High Church, which the school followed. On occasion, I was also responsible for tolling the chapel bell to announce Sunday services. This was just one bell, but it was still tricky to sustain a single tone and not let it sound a double ding.

Miss Evelyn L. Young, was the founding Head Mistress. Fondly known as ELY, she was an imposing woman with short wavy hair and rimless glasses who commanded great respect from all her staff and students. Starting with the official opening of the school in 1912, she led it through two world wars and made sure that all students abided by the Hill Standard "To be the best that I can with the gifts that I have," supported by the school motto and song: *Luce Magistra* (Light Being the Test). The motto reminded us that an eagle, a symbol of hope and strength representing salvation, has exceptionally sharp eyesight and can look directly into the sun. An eagle stood above the school's shield that featured an eagle below a crown and two roses. Upon graduation we received an eagle pin, which I still have.

An important part of our education was learning that our namesake, Queen Ethelburga, had brought Christianity to the north of England. Miss Gilliat, one of the mistresses, had written a play *The Royal Eagle* recounting the story of our queen. This was performed annually to make sure that all students, old and new, and their parents understood fully the significance of the school's name. One year I played the role of King Edwin, suitably attired with a reddish-brown beard and mustache.

At the urging of my brothers, who felt that my occasional stutter could be cured, my parents enrolled me in private elocution lessons. These lessons fortunately alleviated my stutter and gave me excellent training for public speaking in my adult life. Each year I took an exam in Speech and Drama given by the Associated Board of The Royal Schools of Music. In 1950, I took the Grade Six exam and passed with distinction, which would have qualified me to enter the prestigious Royal Academy of Dramatic Arts in London if I had so wished. The ability to enunciate and project my voice also contributed to participation in many school plays. I enjoyed both acting and directing. Dancing was another pleasurable activity. Although we had no male partners, we learned ballroom dancing as well as modern dance.

During the holidays, social life became busier. The war had ended and although there were many changes, people could finally enjoy partying. I was now a teenager. I joined a tennis club, found new friends and an excellent tournament partner. My second eldest brother, John, six years my senior, had splendid good looks and an alluring charisma. He became my chaperone, taught me about men and sex, and helped me find my footing socially. We both enjoyed dancing and soon established a fun group of friends for parties. I loved dressing up for these occasions, wearing the clothes that Mummy bought me. I didn't have the dazzling looks of my brother, but I was termed "attractive." I had large

Handsome brother John Blair

blue eyes, legs almost as shapely as my mother's, and a slender figure comparable to my average height. My hair had darkened since my childhood and was now medium brown, more often referred to as *mousy*. I always wore it short and for most of my teens I had it permed.

Released from wartime blackouts and restrictions on travel, my parents could indulge in vacations. Traveling to the continent was too expensive, but driving to Scotland offered a wonderful alternative. A favorite place was Peebles, near Edinburgh. We stayed at the renowned early 20th century Peebles Hydro hotel and spa resort that had served as a hospital during both world wars. Set in wooded and hilly countryside with extensive grounds and tennis courts, it provided an idyllic vacation spot and was in comfortable driving distance from Edinburgh, enabling us to attend some of the Edinburgh Festival events. My parents stayed in a large, front-facing room on the main guest room floor, and we children, John, Bob, and I, had rooms on the top floor. We gathered with our parents for breakfast and dinner, but for most of the rest of the day John and I joined a group of other young people and participated in tennis tournaments or explored the countryside. My parents allowed 22-year-old John to borrow the car. A group of young people would pile into the car (no required seat belts in those days) and urge our driver to speed along the quiet country roads. John loved to play games with imaginary people. In 1950, an American comedy-drama, starring James Stewart and Josephine Hull, told the story of a man whose best friend was a *pooka*, a creature of Celtic folklore, represented by a six-foot-tall invisible rabbit named Harvey. John would suddenly stop the car to allow Harvey, the fictional rabbit, to catch up and join us. Other days, without my parents' knowledge, I took rides on the back of a friend's motorcycle. The hotel had a grand ballroom and hired a band for evening dancing. We all dressed up, the ladies in long dresses and the men in suits or kilts, and danced the night way. After the dancing finished and

Romy with group of friends at Peebles Hydro, Scotland

most guests had gone to bed, we often played games and tricks on each other, sometimes managing to get a key to someone else's room and make them an apple-pie bed—a British term for short-sheeting, (folding the top sheet back on itself)—to which we sometimes added a prickly hair brush or other tactile object. I also learned what snogging and petting was about—fortunately all reasonably innocent.

During vacations, I enjoyed tennis and parties and dated a few boys from our neighborhood. Certainly, my parents took an interest in my friends and were usually accepting of my activities, except for one time when I experienced the full wrath of my father. I had been on a double date with Tim, a young man from a well-respected family—someone that my mother would certainly have approved of as a suitable husband. Four of us had driven to Scarborough for the day, ending up at a dance hall. I remember jitterbugging with such exuberance that a beautiful, antique bracelet of ammonite stones inherited from my grandmother flew off my wrist and broke into many pieces. I still have the pieces tucked away in a box hoping that someday I can afford to have them glued back together. After dropping off the other couple, Tim and I drove to my house but didn't go in. Instead, we sat in the car and chatted and kissed. It was well into the early hours of the morning by the time Tim drove away and I went into our house. Although I tried to be as quiet as a mouse, my father heard me. The next morning, he tackled me about my lateness, but he was mostly upset that I had sat with a man in a car outside our house. "What would the neighbors think?" he asked. He was so mad that he didn't speak to me for three days. This is the only time I can recall that my father reprimanded me.

Although my published writing career didn't start until I was in my mid-sixties, its genesis occurred in 1949 when I won Queen Ethelburga's Kennedy Essay prize and received a copy of the *Oxford Companion to English Literature*. My 1,000-word essay was titled: "Sermons in Stones." In contrast to a typical spoken sermon which can be often dull, I suggested that carved stones, like those found in churches, temples, pyramids, and even simple undecorated stones found on the ground, may provide the viewer with countless stories and lessons. The composition finished with a quotation from Shakespeare's *As You Like It*:

> *And this our life, exempt from public haunt,*
> *Finds tongues in trees, books in the running brooks,*
> *Sermons in stones, and good in everything.*

In my last years at Queen Ethelburga's I was a Prefect and had the responsibility of making sure the students followed the school rules, didn't wear nail polish, and kept their hair "off their collars" or tied back. In 1948 at the age of 16, I took the Joint Matriculation Board School Certificate in seven subjects: English Language, English Literature, Scripture, Latin, Mathematics, Biology, and Art. My original intent was to spend one year in the Sixth Form and then leave in 1949. I had ambitions to attend art college, a subject for which I seemed to have a special gift, but my parents objected, fearing that it would expose their daughter to an inappropriate Bohemian culture. I also considered going to a finishing school on the Continent. However, two events changed my path: first, a doctor friend of my father's, who occasionally took me out to tea during visitors' weekends, recommended that

I consider university—it would complete my education and still allow me to pursue art later; second, my esteemed head mistress, Miss Young, called me into her office and asked if I would stay on one more year to be head girl. She was about to retire, having been at the school for 39 years, and wanted someone she could trust to help with the transition to a new head mistress—Miss Kerr. How could I refuse? I had great respect for Miss Young, and it was such an honor to be asked to be head girl, and made my father extremely proud.

After two years in the Sixth Form, I received a Certificate of Merit listing the seven subjects I had taken: Divinity, English Literature, History, Latin, Diction, French, and Art. In 1950, I took the Joint Matriculation Board Higher School Certificate (similar to a high school diploma in the United States) and reached the subsidiary standard in English Literature, History, Latin, and Art for which I received a 98% grade. In 1951, I received Advanced ranking in English Literature and History, and Ordinary level in French. The fact that I only took Latin and French at the subsidiary level would prove an impediment when I went on to university. I graduated from Queen Ethelburga's in July 1951.

Queen Ethelburga's School, which had 180 students in my last year, is, at present, Queen Ethelburga's Collegiate with 1,600 students. It is listed as an independent boarding and day school for girls and boys from three months to 19 years old. In 1991, the school left the Woodard Foundation and was purchased by Brian Martin, owner of Equine and Livestock (E & L) Insurance Company. Martin moved the operation to his family home, Thorpe Underwood, near Little Ousebum, northwest of York.

The mottos remain the same, and the school crest still features an eagle. In 1999, Martin converted the senior school into a co-educational enterprise with pupils enrolled from over 30 countries and the reputation of being the most expensive independent boarding school in the United Kingdom. In 2015, Martin's daughter, Amy Martin, became chair of governors.

5. ST. ANDREWS

St. Andrews by the Northern Sea,
A haunted town it is to me!
A little city, worn and grey,
The Grey North ocean girds it round,
And o'er the rocks, and up the bay,
The long sea-rollers surge and sound.
—Andrew Lang from "Almae Matres"

In applying to universities, I put all my eggs into one basket—the University of St. Andrews, Scotland. I wanted a portion of my education to be in Scotland. My father was Scottish and had graduated from the University of Edinburgh and the Royal College of Surgeons, Edinburgh; and my brothers went to Fettes College, a tough, prestigious boys' boarding school in Edinburgh. Though there was some suggestion that I should apply to one of the women's colleges at Oxford or Cambridge, I knew that I didn't have the intellect for such high-caliber institutions.

The name of the town of St. Andrews has its origins in a legendary tale of a fourth century Greek monk, called Regulus, who had been commanded by an angel to take relics of the apostle St. Andrew—an arm bone, a knee-cap, three fingers and a tooth—to the "ends of the earth." Although Regulus' ship was wrecked, he managed to struggle ashore. In gratitude for his life, he gave the name of his patron to the place where he landed.

Following Oxford and Cambridge universities in England, St. Andrews is the third-oldest university in the United Kingdom and the English-speaking world. It was founded in 1410 when a group of Augustinian clerics established a society of higher learning in St. Andrews offering lectures in divinity, logic, philosophy, and law. The emphasis on divinity was especially fitting as St. Andrews already had a monastery and was the seat of the largest bishopric in Scotland. In 1411 Bishop Henry Wardlaw granted the new school a charter of incorporation, and in 1413 persuaded exiled Pope Benedict XIII, supported by the imprisoned King James I of Scotland, to issue a papal bull granting university status to the fledging group. One of the six papal bulls is stored in the university archives. The university grew rapidly: St. Salvator's College was established in 1450, St. Leonard's College in 1511, and St. Mary's College in 1537. By 1579 it was determined that St. Leonard's and St. Salvator's (later combined into United College) would focus on Philosophy or Arts, and St. Mary's on the study of Theology. Some of the original buildings are still being used today.

During the university's 600th celebration in 2011, Professor Louise Richardson, principal and vice-chancellor, described St. Andrews as "remote, isolated, and elemental with ever-changing skies, lengthy winter nights, and endless summer days." Just as St. Regulus thought that St. Andrews was the "end of the earth," students and visitors sometimes think the same. A traveler to St. Andrews soon realizes that he or she is not traveling beyond it—the town is literally the end of the line. A north-bound train from Edinburgh stops at Leuchars Junction where a small train waits on a side line to take riders to St. Andrews. The train passes through green fields before traversing a gorse-encircled golf course bordered on the far end by the ocean. After disembarking from the train, a visitor soon discovers the town of St. Andrews. Wind-swept gray stone buildings cling to the north-facing cliffs of St. Andrews Bay, with the restless ocean wrapping two sides of the town. In the distance the

Map of St. Andrews

Cairngorm Mountains can be seen on a clear day. Three main streets, parallel to the north shore, run in an east-west direction converging at the ruins of the 12th century monastery at the eastern end. Here, down a steep slope lies a long, two-level stone pier protecting the harbor from waves pounding in from the north. Linking the main streets, North Street, Market Street, and South Street are narrow roads and wynds (a narrow lane between houses, typical of many Scottish towns).

Having been unsuccessful in finding accommodation in a university residence hall, I spent my first year in a "bunk" on Murray Street, running between the west end of North Street and the Scores. A bunk was a residence whose owners housed students in shared bedrooms. The landlords provided breakfast and dinner and, during summer recess, rented their bedrooms to vacation visitors. I shared a room with Vicky Robertson, whom I had met at a school Lacrosse match. I was playing for Queen Ethelburga's, and Vicky was a member of the Harrogate Ladies College team. Most bunks had six to eight students, and we soon made friends with first-year arts students who lived on the same street. It was a brisk uphill walk to our classes in the main quadrangle buildings, and we were thankful for the warmth of our obligatory red wool gowns. I took classes in English, French, and Latin, which was mandatory for students taking an Arts degree. Although I started out sitting near the front of the lecture hall and paying close attention to the professor, I was soon invited by a new boyfriend and his colleagues to sit in the higher benches where it was tempting to write notes to each other and pay less attention to the instruction. When it came time to study for exams at the end of the first year, I realized that I lagged far behind in the required reading and had not paid enough attention to the French and Latin exercises. It also became clear that I should have taken these subjects at the advanced level in boarding school.

Two semesters known by their historic names—Martinmas (from September to December), and Candlemas (from February to May)—make up the academic year. The name Martinmas is associated with the feast of St. Martin of Tours, a fourth century bishop and hermit; Candlemas is associated with the feast of the Purification which was celebrated by candlelit processions. During term time the students—about 1,000 in my day—faculty and staff formed over one-third of the town's population. Buildings range from gray stone historic structures in the old town to modern functional classrooms and residence halls in the new town. The heart of the school lies on the northern border of North Street with a quadrangle formed by the 15th century late Gothic chapel on one side and ancient academic buildings on the other sides. On Sundays most of us attended morning service. Mary Auten, who became one of my best friends, was in the choir and felt honored to sing in such a historic building. When the Church of St. Salvator's was consecrated in October 1450, it was the center of the academic and monastic life of the university until 1560 when the Reformation Church removed its decorations and terminated services. It stood unused until 1761 when students and townspeople began to attend again. In the 19th century the church was refurbished and most of its medieval splendor was restored, including the tomb of founder Bishop James Kennedy (1408–1465), which is one of the most elaborate medieval funerary monuments to have survived in Scotland. In 1904 it became the University chapel. For the 550th anniversary of the Chapel in 2010, four new bells were added to the original two which had been recast more than once. Now there are six bells to provide musical challenges for change ringers.

After chapel, with the bells sounding their clarion call across the town, it was traditional for the red-gowned students to parade down to the harbor and walk the length of the pier. Depending on the wind and one's fearlessness, some students walked back along the top of the high part, trying to focus on the pier's stones rather than the wave-swept rocks below.

University was a new experience with unbridled freedom for a young woman who had spent 11 years in regimented girls' boarding schools. There were no parents and no teachers to keep my nose to the grindstone and make sure I did my homework. Course work

St. Andrews harbor and pier

was set by advisors, but it was up to each student to attend classes, study, and do occasional tests. Examinations in each subject were only given at the end of the academic year. Having grown up with three brothers I felt at ease in male company, but now I saw men in a new light. Evidently, they found me attractive, and it was easy to make friends, meet for coffee, or go to the movies. Every Saturday night there was a student "hop" (dance) at the Student Union. I was a good dancer and enjoyed making new friends and being "walked home" and kissed goodnight on the doorstep. Having been a member of the First lacrosse team at Queen Ethelburga's, I had no difficulty qualifying for the university lacrosse team as well as the Scottish Universities team. This required both practice several afternoons a week and matches on most Saturdays. Sometimes the matches were in St. Andrews, but often we had to take an early morning train to Aberdeen, Glasgow, or Edinburgh. Scottish University matches sometimes took place in cities in England, requiring several days away.

Another activity that carried over from boarding school was participation in the university's Mermaid Dramatic Society. My school drama experience, my trained elocution voice, and willingness to participate proved to be ideal credentials. The first play of the year was *Major Barbara* by George Bernard Shaw. I played Barbara Undershaft (Major Barbara). The producer was Kenneth Brice, one of several more mature students who had done their national service before entering university. I am sure I learned my lines and spoke them well, but reviews were critical both of the play's selection as the first play of the year, and my performance: "Barbara as portrayed by Rosemary Blair was convincing when she was concerned with the gentler and more emotional things, but there was little evidence of the strength of character that Barbara was meant to have, so that the taming of Bill Walker assumed the status of a minor miracle." I recall never reading the whole play, resulting in a lack of understanding of Shaw's message and characterizations. For the second play, William Congreve's *The Way of the World,* I was assistant producer and played the role of Mrs. Marwood. In both performances, my good friend, Gillian (Jill) Rees, shone in her roles as Lady Britomart Undershaft and

St. Andrews red-gowned students walking along the pier

Mrs. Millamant. After graduating from St. Andrews, Jill continued to participate in regional theatre in the London area.

Being an active member of The Mermaid was fun, stimulating, and time consuming. In addition to learning our lines and rehearsing, we partied, not just after successful performances but often on a Friday night. I learned what "burning the candle at both ends" meant when after a late night I had to get up early the next morning to catch 7:00 A.M. train for a Lacrosse match. The residence halls and bunks had strict rules about being in by a certain hour. I made a serious breach of the curfew when, after a Mermaid party, my date walked me back to my bunk in the early hours of the morning. Not surprisingly, the front door was locked. But I found a window open and, with the help of my companion, I climbed in only to be met by a very angry landlord who told me that he was going to inform my parents of my behavior.

St. Andrews Lacrosse team. Romy (front row second from right)

Students soon discover that their years at St. Andrews University, set amid medieval ruins and surrounded by rolling countryside and a rugged coastline, are an unforgettable, enchanting experience only to be rediscovered when visiting again after graduation. The historic ruins on the doorstep of the academic buildings were great places to study, take a walk alone, or visit with a boyfriend. In the northeast corner of the old town are the ruins of a castle dating back to the 12th century. The castle served as a palace for the wealthy bishops when St. Andrews was the ecclesiastical center of Scotland. It is situated on a rocky promontory facing the North Sea with a beach below appropriately called Castle Sands. The original form of the castle is still clear with sturdy stone walls and turrets surrounding an open grass covered courtyard. One of the turrets features a toilet with a stone seat and hole dropping down to the ocean below. A mine begun in 1546 and a counter-mine—tunnels cut through solid rock to protect the castle from a siege—still exist and are open to the public today.

Through the centuries the castle was rebuilt several times and, during the Wars of Scottish Independence, changed hands between the Scots and the English. Several famous figures spent time at the castle: James I of Scotland (1406–1437) received part of his education from Bishop Wardlaw, the founder of the university; and James III of Scotland was born there in 1445. Other renowned citizens were imprisoned in the infamous bottle dungeon, a terrifyingly dark, dank hole in the shape of a bottle cut out of solid rock in the north-west tower. It was well barricaded so that students could only threaten others with being dropped into the cavernous space but never actually carry out such a misdeed. Mike Graham, a serious first-year boyfriend, used to take me canoeing along the north shore; sometimes, at low tide, we visited caves under the castle cliffs hoping to find some relic of bygone days. We would launch the canoe from below the Scores, a street bordering the north shore and also where Professor Erskine Wright, Dean of Arts, lived. His sharp eyes spotted us on several occasions, later reprimanding me for spending time with boys when I should have been studying.

The ruins of the Cathedral and St. Rule's tower are synonymous with St. Andrews. The grounds contain the gray sandstone ashlar tower of St. Regulus (St. Rule) at 108-feet high, and a small quire (choir)—all that remain of an older Romanesque-style church and the possible location of the bones of St. Andrew. In 1158 work began on a grand cathedral to be the seat of the Archdiocese of St. Andrews and the center of the medieval Catholic Church in Scotland. After 160 years of construction, it was finally consecrated in 1318 with King Robert the Bruce in attendance. In 1559 John

Knox and his Scottish reformers destroyed the cathedral and removed all its fittings and finery. Now only two western towers and one eastern tower remind us of the original central tower and six turrets. Many of the cathedral's stones were used in later buildings around town. As students, it was a steep but

Romy and Mike Graham 1952

86

easy climb to the top of St. Rule rewarded by 360-degree views of the town and winding coastline. Adjacent to the cathedral is another religious site, the Church of St. Mary on the Rock (St. Mary's College) built in 1537. In her welcome remarks for the 2015 St. Andrews Chronicle, Principal and Vice-Chancellor Louise Richardson spoke of her emotional experience when she joined members of the town and the university at St. Mary's College to break bread at sunrise in celebration of Easter.

The students hold several events to recall the university's history—and as excuses to party. Every year the Kate Kennedy Club—an elite Gentleman's Club whose purpose was to raise money for charities and maintain the university traditions—stages a pageant featuring characters and events from Scottish history. A pipe band leads the procession with costumed individuals representing golfers, clerics, scholars, monarchs, and courtiers, some walking, some on horseback parade down North and Market Streets. One year my future husband Pete, dressed in medieval robes and armor, played the role of King Robert the Bruce. Afterward, the horse that Pete rode in the parade collapsed and died. Bringing up the rear of the procession is a flower-bedecked horse-drawn carriage with a male student dressed as Kate accompanied by her uncle Bishop Kennedy. The often-riotous event has survived frequent attempts by the city to ban it.

The Student's Association holds a Charities Campaign to raise money for various charities, selected each year by the Association. The event includes a parade with groups of students dressed up in different themes, walking, or riding on a float. Raisin Sunday takes place every November to recognize the university tradition of every first-year student (*bejant* or *bejantine*) having a senior man and a senior woman who stand in as their "parents" and help them acclimate to student life. At the beginning of the first year, a senior man would often take his *bejantine* to her first formal ball. The names *Bejant* (male) and *Bejantine* (female) are derived from the French *bejaune* or *bec jaune*, meaning yellow beak or young bird, and used at university to represent a novice or inexperienced person. Traditionally, *bejants* and *bejantines* would visit their senior men and women for tea, taking as a gift a bag of raisins. But the raisins soon translated into wine or other alcoholic beverages and became an excuse for partying. My senior man was a third-year pre-med student named Alec Eason, and my senior woman was the daughter of the well-known children's author Edith Blyton.

My first year had been full of exciting activities: acting, lacrosse, many new friends, and partying. I had certainly become integrated into university life but not into the main reason for attending St. Andrews—the academic life. I dutifully took examinations in my subjects: English, French, and Latin but to my shock I only passed in English. After intensive summer study including an exchange program with a French student, I re-sat French and Latin in September. Again, I failed—by only one point in French. In disgust (mostly with myself) I gave up French but Latin was a requirement so I had to take it again the next year. When I returned in the Fall, the Dean of Arts—the one who lived on the Scores and had seen me enjoying the company of my boyfriend—called me to his office and gave me an ultimatum: If I wanted to continue my studies I must give up the Mermaid and cut back on how much time I spent dating.

6. THE HOME OF GOLF

"Welcome to St. Andrews Links, the Home of Golf. With seven golf courses, we are the largest public golf complex in Europe."
—www.standrews.com

For our second year, four of us—Mary Auten, Jill Rees, Vicky Robertson, and I—decided to rent a flat. We found a three-story house at No. 5 Gibson Place, a little farther west than Murray Park where we had stayed in bunks for the first year. The front of the house opened onto Gibson Place but backed onto a pathway called The Links that bordered the 18th fairway of the Old Course. From our living room window, we had an uninterrupted view across the Old Course to the Royal and Ancient Golf Club and the ocean beyond. Although it could be a steep and windy walk or bicycle ride up to the main quad, the location of the flat was spectacular. Three of us had bedrooms on the top floor with Jill ensconced in a larger room adjacent to our living room on the second floor. The living room boasted a piano, enabling Mary to practice her singing. We shared a basement kitchen and ground-floor bathroom with the landladies who were two elderly Scottish sisters. When we moved in, they instructed us firmly never to sit in the walled-in garden facing the golf course because a third sister had been killed there by a stray golf ball. They were kind and kept to themselves, but we were well aware that they watched over our activities, peeking behind lace curtains and an aspidistra plant at the front window. Occasionally, they would express approval or disapproval of a boyfriend and encouraged us to keep them at a distance and say goodnight on the doorstep. Surprisingly, the landladies did allow us to entertain, but they would reproach us for the number of times the toilet was flushed, adding that our friends must have been drinking excessively.

Following the stern recommendations of the Dean, Professor Erskine Wright, I reluctantly gave up being a Mermaid, but I did continue to play for the First X Lacrosse team and the Scottish Universities team, and participate in all the social activities of the university. There was no shortage of boyfriends. My first-year love, Mike Graham, shared a flat with another student just behind Gibson Place. Fortunately, contact with them was somewhat restricted because the entrance to their flat was from The Links pathway, which required walking up to the next cross street before reaching Gibson Place. After going steady for a year, Mike and I had become unofficially engaged. However, our relationship was often turbulent with angry arguments, one time resulting in my throwing shoes at Mike as he retreated down the stairs from my room. Part way through my second year we split up but remained on good terms.

Being situated in such a small, remote town forced the university to create its own entertainment and social life. At the beginning of every year a "Coming-Up Hop" attended by most students was held in the Younger Hall, a large assembly hall near the main quadrangle, used for dances, entertainment, and graduations. During the year there were several formal dances—formal meaning black tie or kilts for the men, and long ball gowns for the women. The main formals were: Men's Union, Women's Union, Sallies (St. Salvator's residence hall), St. Reg's (St. Regulus residence hall), the Bute Medical Ball, Charities (following Charities fancy dress parade), and the KK Fancy Dress Ball (following the Kate Kennedy parade). Three or four years of formals created quite a challenge for ball gowns. I had several different dresses and had my mother's dressmaker do them over or add sashes or other adornment to make them look different.

The fancy dress occasions tested our ingenuity to create something fun. We usually chose a theme and dressed accordingly. One year for the KK Fancy Dress dance, Mary, Jill, and I were the three loves from Jacques Offenbach's *Tales of Hoffman*; another year I went as Chamber Music, wearing a dress with music symbols on it and a necklace of chamber pots. France and French seemed to have been a popular theme for Charities Day. In 1952, we made a float into a French café and cabaret, but I think we ended up looking more like ladies in a brothel than dancers in a night club. In 1954, a group of us, including some of the men, were can-can dancers, wearing lacy petticoats under our skirts and kicking up our legs as we paraded down Market Street.

The 1953 summer term concluded with an unusual adventure. Accompanied by a young man from my home town—John Stewart was a good friend but not a boyfriend—I decided to hitchhike the 475 miles to London for the coronation of Queen Elizabeth II on June 2. In those days, hitchhiking was not considered as dangerous as it is today but it was still a risky activity for a well-brought-up young lady. It helped that I was not alone and that my companion was male. It also facilitated John catching

Kate Kennedy Fancy Dress – Jill Rees, Romy, Mary Auten

Charities day – cancan dancers

rides when I stood on the curb and did the "thumbing." We did secure a few rides in cars but most of the way we rode in lorries (trucks). I took only a small suitcase and John had a backpack. We managed to find some refreshments between rides and arrived in London after a long 10-hour or more journey.

I knew the address of my eldest brother George who was working in London doing medical research on lop-eared rabbits. I hadn't told him I was coming, so he was none too pleased when he answered the doorbell. It was early in the morning, and he hadn't told his family that he was living with his girlfriend. However, he did usher me in, allow me to take a bath, and provide me with some food. I had arranged with John Stewart to join him and some other St. Andrew's students in St. James' Park alongside the mall, which runs from Trafalgar Square via Admiralty Arch to Buckingham Palace. We thought this would be a good place to wait overnight for the Coronation Procession and the Queen's golden coach to drive down the mall the next day. There were portable toilets in the park and we had blankets to keep us warm and sandwiches and chocolates to appease our hunger.

It was an unforgettable experience to be part of the British crowds passing the long night hours singing and cheering the many entertainers who helped keep the crowds happy. The preamble to the Procession started soon after 9:00 A.M. leading, finally, to the drive-by of the Queen and The Duke of Edinburgh in the Gold State Coach drawn by eight gray geldings and accompanied by footmen and attendants in the full regalia of a royal occasion. Two hundred fifty people, including church leaders, Commonwealth Prime Ministers, members of the Royal Household, civil and military leaders, and the Yeoman of the

Guard made up the rest of the procession. The Queen was only 25 when her father, George VI, died on February 6, 1952 of lung cancer while she was traveling in Africa. The coronation took place in Westminster Abbey and was the first ever to be televised. Few households had televisions, but public locations and public houses (pubs) did. We could have seen so much more if we had watched it on television, but it was so exciting to be part of the large crowds on the streets, parks, and squares of London. It was hard to see much above the mass of people in front of us, but with the help of cardboard telescopes we managed glimpses of the coach and the processions to the abbey and back to the palace. At the end of the exciting day, I went back to my brother's flat and phoned my parents to let them know I would be arriving by train in Hull the next day. I didn't tell them how I got to London. When they met me at the train station, my mother asked why I had such a small suitcase, followed by a quick rejoinder from my father:

"Did you by chance hitchhike to London?"

"Yes, I did. I went with John Stewart, whom you know." Sounding shocked and annoyed my mother replied: "I never thought a daughter of mine would hitchhike."

In addition to the university, St. Andrews is considered to be the home of golf. It is not known when or where the game of golf actually started, but initiation was probably about 1413, the same time as the founding of the university. However, in the early 15th century, James II of Scotland banned golf because it interfered with his men practicing archery. The ban was upheld by James III but was later rescinded by James IV because he himself became a golfer. In 1552, Archbishop John Hamilton, chancellor of the university, granted the townspeople of St. Andrews the right to play on the links. In 1754 a group of noblemen and professors founded The Society of St. Andrew's Golfers, later to become the Royal and Ancient Golf Club. This is still the governing body of golf throughout the world, except in the United States and Mexico.

Between the ocean and the west end of the town, there are four courses huddled together: Old, New, Edens, and Jubilee. Three other courses, Balgove, Strathtyrum, and Castle complete golf links in the vicinity of St. Andrews. The Old Course, which our flat overlooked, is considered to be the home of golf. As students we were privileged to play on the New, Edens, and Jubilee for one pound (sterling) a year. All the courses were beautiful, rugged, and challenging with many yellow-blooming, spikey, gorse bushes bordering rough grass, small streams crossed by stone bridges, and the everpresent wild ocean providing unexpected weather conditions and a fatal destination for lost balls. The 17th "Road Hole" on the Old Course is deemed the hardest hole in tournament golf. Driving to the tee includes a blind shot over some old railway sheds, a notorious sand trap known as the "Road Bunker," a tarmac roadway, and an old stone wall. On Sundays, the Old Course rests with no play permitted. For us, the areas around the courses were perfect for afternoon strolls with some of the shelters making ideal locations for romantic visits at night. Alongside the Jubilee and New Courses, the curve of St. Andrews Bay creates a two-mile stretch of broad sands backed by dunes and high grass. The opening and closing scenes in the movie *Chariots of Fire* shows a group of athletes running along the West Sands at the edge of the water with speckles of wet sand hitting their shirts. Their race toward the city, discernable by the Royal and Ancient Clubhouse and red sandstone mass of the Grand Hotel (Hamilton Hall in our day), has left an indelible mark on students' memories.

Many tournaments are played at St. Andrews, including the celebrated Open Tournament played on the Old Course every five years. Toward the end of 1954, during our stay at 5 Gibson Place, the first of several Commonwealth Tournaments was held to celebrate the bicentenary of the royal and Ancient Golf Club with teams from Great Britain, Australia, Canada, New Zealand, and South Africa. They were all top golfers, young, bronzed, and handsome. We had front row seats from our flat, but it was more fun to walk the course and follow the players, especially as the sun was shining with a light breeze, making it ideal golfing weather. I chose a South African player to follow because I liked the look of him. He was tall and wiry with dark wavy hair and eyes as brown as mahogany. Enjoying the salty smell of the sea air, I followed my chosen player, Alan, the full round of the course. He made a good score, slightly spoiled by a bunker shot at the infamous Road Hole. At the end of the round, to my surprise, he came up to me, saying my name:

"Hello Romy, did you enjoy the play today?"

It was such a serendipitous moment. I was attracted to him and he to me, having picked me out from all the spectators, and finding out my name from his student caddy. Alan invited me and my flat mates to the players' party at the Rusacks Hotel, one of several hotels in the vicinity of the Old Course. The evening passed pleasantly with the raucous laughter of golfers shattering the sedate atmosphere of the historic hotel. As Alan walked me home he asked:

"Can I see you again after play tomorrow?"

After dinner, Alan took me for a drive following the rugged coastline to somnolent Crail. On our way back, we stopped on the headland to enjoy the view of lights twinkling against the dark sky and shadowy outline of the gray stone town. We sat in the car for a while enjoying each other's company. But Alan, conscious of his player responsibilities, had to get back for a good night's sleep before an early start the next day to journey to the Continent for another tournament. He promised to stay in touch and call me.

Term was over, and I went home for the summer but, as always, with studying to do for some repeat exams in September. One day the phone rang. After answering it, Mother called:

"Rosemary, there is a call for you from Paris."

Paris! We never received overseas phone calls, and who did I know in Paris? To my surprise it was Alan, my South African golfer friend.

"Hello Romy, how are you? Can you tell me the name of the perfume you use?"

I told him, thinking how thoughtful of him to buy me some perfume.

"How is your tour going?" I asked.

"Great. I expect to be back in England soon, and I will get in touch with you," Alan responded.

A couple of weeks later Alan phoned from Manchester: "Hello. I am now in Manchester for a tournament. Would you like to come over and watch the play?"

I replied: "Oh, I would love to but my parents would never allow me to use one of their cars. Besides, I am supposed to be studying for some exams."

Three days later the doorbell rang. There was Alan, who had borrowed a car and come to see me before returning to South Africa. I was thrilled. We went out to dinner and then drove around, stopping as we had before to kiss and cuddle. Again, Alan had to cut his visit short. He had 100-mile trip back to rejoin his team and catch a morning flight. As we were saying goodnight he said:

"Thank you so much for telling me the name of your perfume. I bought some to take back to my girlfriend in South Africa."

I was devastated, having expected that the purchase was for me! In hindsight, I should have been flattered that he wanted to retain a memory of me when he returned to his own country and his steady girlfriend.

As a retreat from both studies and university life, I took an occasional weekend break to visit a cousin of my father's who lived in Crail, a short bus ride south of St. Andrews. The Reverend George Blair was a graduate of St. Andrews and a retired Minister of the Church of Scotland. He was widowed and lived in a house called Corner Croft perched on a promontory beyond the small harbor of Crail. From every window in the house you could see the ocean. It was a dramatic setting, but when there was a storm and the wind blew you felt that the house might not stay upright.

A few steps from the house it was possible to walk down to the rocky shore below and search for shells or small sea creatures. My visits to Cousin George would always include a bus ride to some church where he might be the visiting preacher, or a brisk walk around Crail harbor, or along the cliffs. It was a therapeutic time. A chance to blow away the cobwebs, get life into perspective, and feel refreshed after interesting discussions with an erudite but humble man. I stayed in touch with him after I graduated and kept him informed of my post-graduate life. In one of his replies he wrote: "Your brief visits to me at Crail will always be treasured memories."

For Arts students, St. Andrews awarded only Masters of Arts (MA) degrees, either with Honors or a simple MA. I had started my university career with the ambition of taking Honors English, a four-year program. Having messed up by failing two classes in my first year, I had to change course and adjust my subjects both in the second and third years. For my second year I took required General Philosophy (Logic and Metaphysics), Latin again, and General Modern History. I finally passed Latin on my third attempt in September but having given up French I was still short of the required credits to continue toward my degree. Therefore, for my third year, as well as taking Special Modern History and Special English Literature and Language which involved studying Middle English—only slightly easier than Anglo-Saxon which would have been a requirement if I had taken Honors English—I had to add a third subject: General Economic History. I should have graduated with a regular MA at the end of the third year but again I still lacked the necessary credits. This meant that, if I wanted a degree, I had to return for a fourth year (my planned

Honors year) to take a second round of Special Modern History and Special English Language and Literature as a combined English-History degree.

I was very aware that I had disappointed my parents, but my father was surprisingly supportive, telling me that he admired my grit and persistence. Failing exams seemed to be a family problem. In spite of their intelligence, all three brothers struggled with exams. George had to take his MRCP (Membership of the Royal Colleges of Physicians) examination more than once. John, having achieved a degree in Chinese, was unable to pass the English test for acceptance to the British Foreign Office. As a replacement, he obtained a job with Matheson & Company's tea trade division, living in India for a few years before returning to England and finding positions in personnel management for several different companies. Bob's headmaster at Fettes College advised my father that his youngest son was not "university material." Instead, Bob attended a technical school in Hull and became a highly-skilled draftsmen, working for Blackburn Aircraft Limited all his life. Obviously, my problem was a lack of focus on academic studies. As it happened, my fourth year would yield an unexpected development.

7. PETE

*"He [Pete] is one of the most gifted persons who at an early age seem to have
come to terms with life both naturally and easily; he is mature without loss of
youthfulness, industrious without pedantry . . . and at our parties he would 'go
to town' with an unrivalled exuberance."*
—Mike Banks in "High Arctic"

Our enjoyable stay at No. 5 Gibson Place had come to an end.
Vicky had given up pursuit of a degree and left after the
second academic year to marry Sandy McGraw, an attractive and
rakish son of a Scottish minister. After the third academic year,
Jill graduated with a standard MA and returned to London, and
Mary moved into a residence hall to concentrate on studying for
her Honors MA in History. Not having planned to return for
a fourth year, I was suddenly at a loss to find lodging. Another
fourth-year student, Lorna, came to my rescue. There was an
available bedroom in the flat that she was renting from a Miss
Pettigrew. The bedroom was small, but I was allowed to use
Lorna's larger room when she was not entertaining or for meals.

During my third year I had started going out with a student
who was doing his pre-medical courses in St. Andrews. Andy
Dewar was a fun-loving, fresh-faced, handsome Scotsman. At the
beginning of my fourth year, he had moved to Dundee, the center

for advanced medical classes. We saw each other but less frequently than when he was residing in St. Andrews. During the first term, Andy invited me to the Bute Medical Ball in Dundee. I was thrilled to go and was able to stay overnight with Rita Dando, a friend from Mermaid days, who was doing a post-graduate teaching course in Dundee. Like other university balls, it was an enjoyable evening with both ballroom and Scottish country dancing, which I especially enjoyed and was able to do well. Afterward, Andy walked me back to the flat and came in for some snogging. We knew that we were risking the landlady's disapproval so we tried to be extremely quiet, but the couch, which folded out into a bed, was old and creaked with the slightest movement. Within a short time, there was a loud banging on the door. It was an irate landlady shouting:

"I know you have a man in there. He must leave immediately or I will phone the police."

Andy slunk out as quietly and quickly as he could. I left early the next morning to catch the train back to St. Andrews after paying Rita for the night's charge and expressing hope that the landlady wouldn't take my transgressions out on her.

As well as taking advanced classes in English and History, I had a part-time job working in the library, hand-copying medieval documents recording events and administrative business of the old city of St. Andrews. My Economics History professor had recommended me for the position, probably because I had neat handwriting and was capable of reading Middle English. I felt privileged to work in the library, which was in one of the oldest buildings near St. Mary's College on South Street; but, despite providing some extra cash, the job was quite tedious.

On a Saturday night Lorna and I, and Mary, when she could pull herself away from her books, would frequent the pubs before going on to the Student Union Hop. One evening, not long before the Christmas break, we went to the Cross Keys cocktail bar on Market Street, a popular hangout with the rugby crowd. Before long, a student that I didn't know came up and introduced himself. He had obviously had a few beers, but he seemed very pleasant.

"Hello, my name is Peter Wyllie. I remember you playing Major Barbara in the Mermaid production a couple of years ago. You were very good."

A week or two later, I met him again on a bus outing to a ski location in the Cairngorms north of St. Andrews. I was sitting with Anne Waterman, one of the American exchange students who happened to have Peter Wyllie as her senior man. Because Anne was keen on the man sitting next to Pete, she asked me to exchange places so she could work her charms on him. After meeting Pete in the Cross Keys, I had done some homework to find out more about him. Evidently, he was well known for various reasons but mostly for just having spent two years on an expedition to unexplored territory in North Greenland. Trying to hide the fact that I wasn't at all sure of the location of Greenland, I asked Pete about his expedition. It was like pulling teeth—he was shy and quite reluctant to talk about his unusual adventure. We skied together, but the conditions were deplorable. The snow on the hill—you couldn't call it a mountain—was in patches with coarse grass in between. There was no lift, not even a rope tow, so we took off our skis and walked to the top and took a few tentative runs down where we could find snow. When it was time for lunch, I discovered that Pete hadn't brought anything so I shared my sandwich with him. Little did I know then that I would end up sharing the rest of my life with him.

During the Christmas break, I spurned my parent's expectation that I would spend Christmas at home and seized the opportunity to join a group of American exchange students on a ski trip to Austria. We went to Warth, a tiny village 5,000 feet high in the Vorarlberg area on the northern border of Austria. In 1953, not many skiers knew about Warth, but because of its proximity to Lech, the remote village is now in the front ranks of Austrian ski resorts. We stayed at the Berghotel Biberkopf. Most of us were beginners so we had an instructor who taught us how to ski down a gentle slope and snow plough to break our speed. We used a rope tow to get back to the top. The instructor also took us on cross country trails where we attached strips of seal skin to our skis for walking up the slopes. In the evenings we mingled with some of the villagers, drinking and dancing in the hotel. Klaus, who was considered the best skier in the village, took a liking to me and persuaded me to accompany him on a ski tour of the hills around the village. I don't know how I dared to go with him because he spoke no English and I spoke no German. But I admired his skiing and trusted that he would keep me safe on the slopes. We stopped at a remote farm house where the farmer's wife gave us refreshments, but again I felt helpless because I couldn't communicate except through hand signals and the odd word or two of German which the locals may not have spoken. On our last evening at the hotel, Klaus danced with me all evening and persuaded me to find a remote corner of the hotel where we could kiss and caress. Crazily, I stayed up most of the night and just managed to get my bag packed before we left in the morning. Because of dangerous snow conditions on the road down from the mountain, we had to travel by horse sleigh with a skier going ahead of us to check for avalanches. Klaus said a warm goodbye and made sure the blanket was well wrapped around me on the open sleigh. It was quite an adventure, and I was glad to get away with my life and everything else intact.

Soon after my return to St. Andrews, Pete invited me out. This seemed to be the beginning of a new chapter. Andy Dewar was out of the picture, and Peter Wyllie was my new beau, a tall and well-built Englishman with sandy-brown, wavy hair. We started having regular dates, going to the movies, spending Saturday evening dancing at the Hop, attending some of the formal balls, and meeting in one of the many coffee shops frequented by students. I discovered that Pete was on a tight budget so whenever possible, I paid my way. I also discovered that he had few clothes and that his socks had holes in them. As I

Pete and Romy at St. Salvator's Residence formal ball, St. Andrews

had learned to darn in the early days of boarding school, I offered to darn his socks. We would meet for coffee and exchange holey socks—clean I am glad to say—for newly darned ones.

Somehow my relationship with Pete was different from the friendships I had with other young men. The connection was less of an infatuation and more of a deeper feeling. He seemed to really care for me and was just completely trustworthy and thoroughly nice. We soon became good friends as well as lovers. Gradually, I learned his story. After graduating from Hampton Grammar School in 1948, Pete had won a four-year Residential Scholarship at St. Andrews, which the committee agreed reluctantly to hold until he had completed his compulsory National Service. He joined the Royal Air Force hoping to be sent overseas but, much to his disappointment, after basic training he was stationed at Leuchars Airport near St. Andrews. When not working as a Radio Telephony Operator (RTO), he was able to explore some of the university social activities. It was 1950 when he became a first-year student, enrolling in science classes with plans to take a degree in Physics but soon choosing Geology as his major. Having participated in boxing and soccer as a young boy, followed by rugby and winning the RAF Scotland heavyweight boxing championship in the Air Force, he was well qualified to join the university rugby and boxing teams.

In 1951, during the autumn term of his second year at St. Andrews (aged 21), he ended up at the bottom of a rugby game scrum. The university doctor determined that his neck was merely bruised. After some time off and clearance by the doctor, Pete started training and fought in the heavyweight division of the Scottish Universities Boxing Championships in January 1952, followed soon after by an exhibition bout with an Aberdeen student in St. Andrews. It was now four months since the rugby accident. During the exhibition match, Pete experienced tingling sensations in his arms and fingers. Seriously concerned, he visited a specialist who diagnosed him with dislocation of the neck, and ordered immediate surgery at a hospital in Perth. The surgeon took a piece of bone from Pete's hip to fuse two of his neck vertebrae. He spent several weeks in the hospital in a plaster "coffin" until the doctors were able to fit him with a Madonna cast. This went over his head, neck, and chest with an opening for his face and ears, and stayed in place for five months. Determined to continue his university program, Pete returned to St. Andrews. He studied by lying face down on a bed with books on the floor. For his final B.Sc. exams, he was assigned a portable lectern and was allowed to walk around the exam hall to relieve the strain. Undeterred, he even went to the Saturday night hops where Chris Walker, a good friend, remembers dancing with him because she was tall enough to see over the cast and guide their movements. Some doctors said that Pete would make a full recovery and be able to play rugby and box again. He did make a good recovery but wisely gave up all contact sports.

During his university years, Pete had the opportunity of two adventures in Greenland. The first was in 1950 at the end of his first year. Harald Drever, a Geology professor, invited Pete to join his summer expedition to West Greenland, the first excursion to Greenland since the war ended. The experience included setting up tents on rocky terrain, dragging a sledge across hummocky ice to collect rocks, and Pete, with a rope secured around his waist and chest, being dropped halfway down a crevasse to record the

Pete – Arctic explorer

crystal shapes and textures by taking rubbings of the ice walls.

The second adventure was at the end of his third year when Professor Drever recommended Pete for inclusion with the upcoming British North Greenland Expedition. The 1952–54 expedition, which had been in the planning stages for several years, was led by Commander James Simpson of the Royal Navy, whose book *North Ice* recounted the details of the expedition. The purpose was threefold: to map unexplored land, to gain scientific knowledge, and for members of the services to acquire experience operating in Arctic environments. Simpson was also keen to add to Britain's reputation of Arctic exploration. It was a huge undertaking both in planning, execution, and financing. Three important organizations gave their blessing: The Royal Society, the Royal Geographic Society, and the Scott Polar Research Institute. The bulk of the financial support came from the Shell Oil Company with contributions from several industries and other private companies and individuals. HM The Queen—at that time Princess Elizabeth—agreed to be patron and Sir Winston Churchill was vice-patron. The British government provided staff, equipment, and provisions, and the Air Force provided Sunderland flying boats. During a preparatory exploration in 1951, Simpson had discovered a lake free of ice in Dronning Louise Land where the Sunderlands could land. He named it Britannia Lake. Unable to find a British naval vessel equipped to break through the Arctic ice to get the men and equipment from England to the northeast coast of Greenland, Simpson chartered a Norwegian sealer named the *Tottan*.

The 25-man expedition was made up of two parts: members of the forces, mostly naval personnel, many of whom were mountain climbers and keen to test their skills on the Greenland mountains—this group would provide man power and earn experience in Arctic conditions—and scientists who would study the unexplored northern half of Greenland with particular emphasis on seismic and gravity surveys to test the thickness of the ice sheet and the effect of its weight on the land beneath it. The scientists included meteorologists who would establish weather stations to aid in Arctic flying, and two geologists who would survey and map Dronning Louise Land. The group also included two doctors to look after the men and study how they coped with Arctic conditions, and three radio operators to manage the vitally important radio equipment for communication with home (England) and the various divisions of the expedition as the men spread out to do their work. The scientists working on the ice sheet would use M29 Weasels, a World War II tracked-vehicle capable of negotiating rough Arctic conditions; the geologists would use sledges pulled by husky dogs or man pack (walk with loaded backpacks).

After rigorous interviews by the leaders and the Bishop of Portsmouth, who had been a geologist on Antarctic expeditions, Pete was accepted as the junior geologist. Princess Elizabeth came to Deptford on the south bank of the River Thames to meet the expedition members before they set sail in July 1952 on the *Tottan*. Another ship, carrying the four Weasels, sailed from Hull (my home town). After stops in Reykjavik, Iceland, and south-west Greenland to collect the husky dogs, the *Tottan* had a rough passage through the pack ice before reaching Young Sund on the north-east coast of Greenland. Here the men—Pete was considered especially helpful—unloaded all the gear, supplies, and dogs from the ship to the Sunderland flying boats, which then transported the men and equipment to Britannia Lake. Using pre-fabricated parts purchased in Canada, the men built their base hut on the shores of the lake.

Before winter set in, Commander Simpson led a party with dog sledges to establish a station on the ice cap. The station, which was named North Ice, had its equipment air-dropped by two

HRH Princess Elizabeth inspecting members of the British North Greenland Expedition on the icebreaker Tottan

RAF Hastings transport planes flying from Thule, an American air base in the north-west coastal region. The North Ice residents conducted important glaciological, seismic, and gravimetric work during the two-year period, with one party traversing the ice cap from North Ice to Thule. It took until May of 1953 for the Weasels, which were essential for those working on the ice cap, to reach North Ice. Because of increasing sea ice, the *Tottan* had to leave the vehicles and two drivers at Danmarkshavn, a Danish weather station, where they spent the winter. In the spring the plan was to drive the Weasels to North Ice, via the expedition's base at Britannia Lake. But the challenge of getting them across the Storstrommen, a broad glacier between the coast and the base, proved almost unsurmountable.

Once the base hut had been built, various projects could begin. For instance, Pete and others carried out preliminary surveying and rock collecting. Finding routes across the rough terrain the men, and with 60- to 90-pound packs on their backs, picked up air drops and established supply depots in readiness for spring travel, which would begin once there was enough daylight following the three months of winter darkness. In early March, eager to get out and start their surveying and mapping, the two geologists, Douglas Peacock and Peter Wyllie, set out with their dog team and a two-man tent. The dogs had been purchased in West Greenland the previous year, and Pete became the owner of the team. He told me that the dogs were their servants and companions. He knew each one of them by name and personality, quickly learning to respect the alpha dog. He found out how to cope with the different quirks of each member and how to manage a fight and punish when necessary. All the dog teams were attached to the sledges in a fan formation. This worked well unless a dog decided to change places, causing the driver to have to stop and disentangle their traces.

The geologists' first attempt to travel was hampered by such severe winds that they had to "lay-up" in their tent for several days, finally giving up and returning to base. When they set out for a second time in April, conditions were much better, and they spent the next four and half months traveling, surveying, mapping, taking rock samples, and writing up field notes at night in the shelter of their tents. The cold was intense and conditions could be extremely rough at times. When Pete left for Greenland, a student friend, Chris Walker, the woman who had helped guide him on the dance floor when he was in his plaster cast, offered to write letters and keep him in touch with life at St. Andrews. He wrote a few letters back describing his experiences. As mail was only delivered once a year when the Sunderland flying boats brought supplies in summer, Pete would get a bundle of letters from home and be able to "mail" the letter he had been composing during his long sledging trip. Here are some excerpts from a letter to Chris:

MARCH 4, 1953. I am writing inside a 2-man arctic pyramid tent, with the primus going full blast, the apex of the tent filled with clothing hanging to dry and the walls of the tent caked with ice, and my sleeping bag wet at the top near to the primus [stove], with frozen stuff at my feet. Outside, a wind is howling past, the snow is being whirled along in the vicious cutting drift, and my dog team, fastened to a chain, is almost covered in drift. . . . The temperature outside is –20 degrees Fahrenheit. . . . During our programme of 4.5 months we shall work from a series of depots, which will be laid for us along the west of Queen Louise Land. . . . I cannot remember if you were one of the people who suggested that I would be sleeping with Eskimo girls during the winter, but if so, I must correct you. . . . This is an expedition and we have put aside earthly things. We endure hardships, with no thought of comforts of the flesh. Anyway, the nearest Eskimo settlement is 400 miles away south, on the coast . . . so we are forced to live celibate lives for 2 whole years not even seeing a woman, let alone amusing ourselves with one. The only feminine company I have is the bitch in my team. She is a sweet black little dog with a torn ear, and when I see her flirting with the boys in the team, she quite reminds me of you. Her name is Suik, but she is commonly known as Suet Pudding.

Strange though it may seem . . . I am thoroughly enjoying the life here. After a while, the cold means damn all . . . you soon get used to rubbing your sleeping bag, and head and arms, on the ice on the tent walls . . . the only thing you can't get used to is the wind with low temperatures. Beards are out. The moisture in the breath condenses as ice on the hair of

Pete's dog team, in fan formation, chasing the sledge ahead

the face, and if the beard is long, the ice gets into large lumps matted and tangled in the hair. . . . Instead of a beard I am going in for a long hair style . . . at the present rate I shall look quite girlish in 2 years.

MAY 1, 1953. The effect of the sun and rise in temperature, plus the effect of the primus [stove] at evening and morning has put the ice level in our tent lower to the floor so the walls are dry and bare of ice. . . . It is now a simple matter to melt my ink on the primus in the evenings, hence the more readable writing equipment.

The winter with its low temperatures and darkness did not seem too long. In fact, none of us did half the things we intended during the "long winter darkness.". . . We had a gramophone with hundreds of long-playing records, a laboratory for work, dogs to feed, sledges to mend, a dark room in which I spent much time producing photographs. . . . We had a Highland dancing society.

We are moving up and down the glaciers . . . paying visit to the cliffs collecting rock specimens, and writing up notes in the evenings . . . In the autumn we had to carry everything on our backs. I have one picture wading a glacier stream—water very close to freezing, running straight off the ice, with a 90 lb. pack on my back, and no trousers on. Don't be embarrassed, Chris, my shirt tail is fairly long, and the sun is behind me. . . . During the summer and early autumn sledging is out because everything is melting . . . then we have to man-pack.

I hope this stuff is not boring you too much, but what else can I write about? I have no news from home, and no social activities or flirtations to report. That's your ration for now, I must do some work.

AUGUST 13, 1953. First Sunderland on the lake. I have received your pile of letters, and I shall reply before the last one [plane] leaves.

In spite of North Greenland being an Arctic wilderness, there were occasional sightings of wild life. Pete shot some hares and trapped a couple of white Arctic foxes, which he skinned, saving the furs to bring home. In the summer months there were interesting birds and colorful flowers and the possibility of spotting a polar bear near the coast. Pete also had two terrifying encounters with musk-oxen. The first was during the late summer forays of 1952 when Pete and Ron Moreton were collecting air-dropped rations. Ron Moreton told the story in *North Ice*. On their way back to base, they spent two challenging days crossing a thinly-iced lake to reach some rocks Pete wanted to collect for study during the winter. Just as they sat down to remove their crampons and take a well-deserved rest, Pete saw a huge musk-ox coming toward them. Usually musk-ox shied away from humans but this appeared to be a lone bull, perhaps cast out from the herd. Seeing the two men, the animal let out a roar and started to gallop toward them. With nowhere to shelter, and no time to clip on their crampons, the men raced across the ice to a small hillock where, with trembling fingers, they managed to get their crampons onto their boots. Although the beast had temporarily lost sight of his target, he quickly picked up the chase. As Pete rushed onto the lake, the ice gave way, but with an enormous leap, he reached a safe spot. Ron followed, skirting around the broken area. Fortunately, the fractured ice prevented the still roaring musk-ox from following, and the men lived to tell of their adventure.

The second musk-ox encounter was during October of 1953 when Pete was traveling with George Fletcher, who had joined the Expedition for the second year. This time Pete recorded the unnerving event in *North Ice*. Their work completed, Pete was driving his husky dog team back to base. As he was speeding across an iced lake, Pete saw a large boulder suddenly moving. It was a musk-ox. Soon he spotted three more musk-oxen behind a moraine, just 100 yards away. He quickly jammed the sledge between some rocks so that he could release a couple of his dogs to chase the quarry. He got one dog unhooked and was struggling with the clip of another, when the dogs, who were very hungry and excited, jerked the sledge loose and ran off, dragging not only the sledge across the boulders but Pete as well, stretched out on his back with his feet in front of him and a frightened dog racing alongside him. Hardly aware of the bumpy boulders over which he was being dragged, Pete was more concerned about being bitten by the dog whose traces had caught around his ankle. Finally, he broke free. Without his weight, the sledge and the dogs raced toward the musk-oxen. Now Pete had to worry about the animals' horns puncturing his dogs as they attacked the musk-oxen. As soon as he managed to retrieve his rifle, he shot the musk-oxen before they could do any more harm to his dogs. Somehow, they had escaped any serious injury and were now happily feasting on the slain beasts.

The expedition was an unforgettable experience, one that was toughening both physically and mentally, helping to prepare Pete for future challenges. He had gained incomparable experience in his chosen science, Geology. He had learned to manage a team of husky dogs and survive exceptionally tough conditions. He had endured three winter months of total darkness, twice, and learned to get along with a consortium of 25 men, some of whom were challenging companions and others who became lifelong friends. The group stayed in touch, gathering twice for reunions in Wales and Devon, which we attended.

At the end of the expedition, the sledge drivers sought new homes for their dog teams. Some were flown to the Antarctic to pull sledges in the Falkland Islands Dependencies, some were returned to West Greenland, but unfortunately for a few there was no home because they were too old and would not have survived as pets in a civilized environment. With heart-wrenching sadness and to make the task a little easier, each owner shot another's dogs. Pete kept skins from his two dogs, which we used as costumes when we went to a Kate Kennedy Fancy Dress Dance as cave man and woman. To make my appearance more authentic, a St. Andrew's colleague of Pete lent me a dinosaur bone I wore around my neck. Adorning the floor in his home office, Pete still has the polar bear skin that he used under his sleeping bag in Greenland.

For their participation in the British North Greenland Expedition, Peter and all the members received the Polar Medal from HM The Queen. Pete's mother went with him to Buckingham Palace and observed that, to her surprise, some of the window coverings had holes in them.

St. Andrews Kate Kennedy Fancy Dress — Pete & Romy dressed as cave man and woman

An important aspect of my relationship with Pete was his insistence on studying. He had always been a top student, often winning awards—in 1955 he won the Miller Prize for the most distinguished graduate in the Faculty of Science. He knew of my poor record and wanted to make sure that his friendship didn't interfere with my degree program. Therefore, we had study dates. Most of these took place in his rooms. As the Senior Student of St. Salvator's (Sallies) Residence Hall, Pete was privileged to have a small suite of rooms on the ground floor. Sallies—now co-educational—is famous for being the residence hall where the Duke (Prince William) and the Duchess of Cambridge met in 2001. When Pete lived there it was an all-male residence, and women were only permitted to visit in the common room. However, as Senior Student and with the warden as a neighbor and good friend, Pete felt free to invite me to his rooms. Sitting by a log fire in Pete's sitting room, we would study for a couple of hours, and then finish the evening with some relaxation before Pete walked me back to my bunk. Occasionally, after an evening date to see a movie or enjoy the Saturday hop—Pete was an excellent ballroom dancer having learned as a teenager in London—he would come in to my small room. Knowing that the landlady, Miss Pettigrew, like all Scottish landladies, strongly disapproved of men visiting women in their rooms, we tried to be especially quiet sitting on the floor instead of on the bed.

I had given up Lacrosse to focus on my studies, but Pete and I did play the occasional game of golf, which Pete had taken up after his rugby accident. For all two-handed sports, he played left-handed and had bought a set of used left-handed clubs. I had inherited my mother's wooden clubs. Sometimes we played a one-ball game meaning that we took it in turns to make a stroke. This was unorthodox, but as I was a beginner it helped us get around the course in reasonable time. Pete tended to slice the ball, and I managed to get it back on the fairway. Putting was less of a challenge. Golf enabled us to spend time together enjoying the fresh sea air, usually on the Edens course, which ran parallel to the ocean.

We also enjoyed walks along the West Sands, stopping to snuggle in the shelter of the dunes, or through the historic Lade Braes, an area that was created sometime in the 12th century to transport water to the priory. For most of its early life the lade— or *lead* meaning artificial watercourse—was open, allowing the townspeople to use the water for washing clothes, cleaning fish, and perhaps for drinking. By the middle of the 19th century, the watercourse was covered over and trees and shrubbery planted, making it a picturesque and popular walk.

Graduation was held on July 5, 1955. With Pete's help and mentoring, I had finally passed my exams. According to my scroll: "*Franciscam Rosemariam Blair* received an *Artium Liberalium Magistrum* degree." My parents came to St. Andrews for the occasion. It was a happy day recorded with photographs and a celebratory dinner.

As we endure the hardships and isolation of the 2020 coronavirus epidemic, I am reminded of the joy and satisfaction that graduating from university brought. Along with many students around the world, two of my granddaughters and a grandson have had their college lives cruelly interrupted. One granddaughter and the grandson were able to complete their degree requirements online but had to graduate virtually, missing the fulfillment

Rosemary Blair MA, St. Andrews

of the ceremony, such as tossing mortarboards into the air and breaking open bottles of champagne with family and friends. The other granddaughter unfortunately had to complete her first-year art classes online, and is now in limbo wondering what will happen to the upcoming academic year.

Pete received his B.Sc. degree in 1952 and his B.Sc. Honors in 1955, although he chose not to participate in the degree ceremonies. Following this, he started work on a Ph.D. under the supervision of Professor Drever, leaving Greenland geology for petrological research on Scottish rocks on the island of Soay, just off the coast of Skye. At the same time, he was considering options for his future. One possibility was to accept an offer from Shell Oil Company (his father's firm) to become a geologist for their oil explorations; this would require travel and tough conditions in far-off locations. Another possibility was to follow Drever's suggestion that he pursue geological research at a university. Drever successfully advocated for an assistantship in the laboratory of Professor Frank Tuttle at the Pennsylvania State University in the United States. Because our relationship seemed to be heading toward something permanent, Pete asked me what I thought. If I was to be involved, I recommended the university position. I had already considered going to America on my own where I had a cousin married to an American diplomat, and I didn't like the idea of living in a jungle in some far off South American territory. We agreed that if Pete was going to accept the position in America, it would be a good idea to get married. During the summer we visited Pete's parents in Twickenham, London. During the visit, Pete proposed to me, giving me a lovely diamond and emerald ring we had found in an antique shop on Edinburgh High Street. Afterward we visited my family in Yorkshire, and Mother gave us a grand engagement party.

During my time at St. Andrews, I and my close women friends discussed the question of finding a husband at university. Was it a good idea? Would it happen, and if so, would it be a successful outcome? I felt that marrying someone who had experienced the same learning environment would make my outlook on life too limited. I looked forward to expanding my horizons and meeting men with diverse encounters and qualifications. My plan was to get a degree but not a husband. However, after four years I had the good fortune to obtain not only a degree but a husband, one who came from a different background, who had endured a physical and mentally tough two years in the Arctic, and had a promising academic career ahead of him. Now, together with Pete, I was about to begin a new chapter in my life.

Romy's parents, Mr. & Mrs. Bertram Blair, attending graduation

8. OUR WEDDING

"To have and to hold, from this day forward, for better, for worse,
for richer, for poorer, in sickness and in health, to love and to cherish,
till death do us part...."

Most university graduates today hope that their education is finished and they can find a position in the working world easily. However, even in the mid-1950s, it was often necessary to take some further training, either teacher training or more commonly secretarial instruction. With an MA in English and History, I hoped to find a job as an assistant to a writer, but knowledge of shorthand and typing was essential to have any hope of opening that door. At the end of August, 1955, I enrolled at St. Godric's Secretarial College for Administrative, Secretarial and Allied Careers located in Hampstead, London. I thought it would be exciting to experience life in the British capital. The course, which lasted six months, was designed specifically for college graduates and overseas visitors looking for British training. I found lodging nearby, sharing a room and bathroom with another St. Godric's student.

Romy's engagement portrait

The college had been founded in 1929 by Emily Loveridge. Her son, Sir John Warren Loveridge, who studied engineering at St. John's College, Cambridge, and developed fighter aircraft, became principal of St. Godric's from 1954 until the college closed in 1990. Sir John was also a member of Parliament, a farmer, a published poet, and an abstract sculptor. The college had high standards and provided a useful education, not just in secretarial skills—typing and shorthand—but in proper etiquette required of a good secretary for the corporate world in London and other big cities. I still have a notebook, neatly typed and organized, for a class called "Commercial Practice." It was a detailed treatise on how to conduct business of all kinds: banks, insurance, trade, the stock exchange, income tax, law offices, and other commercial enterprises. The class included instruction in *Qualities Required in a Secretary*: "A Secretary must know how to be tactful and must have a certain amount of charm. She must use initiative, so that she can quietly continue work when the boss is not there." The list of requirements included Reliability, Discretion, Loyalty, Helpfulness, Exactitude, and Patience. Appearance, neatness, and punctuality were important with bright red nail polish and lipstick deemed inappropriate. In addition to typing letters, we had to learn how to address a variety of people ranging from the queen, royal dukes, princes, princesses, and all the various titles of the aristocracy; judges for different courts, the ranks of clergy in the English Church and the Catholic Church, and civic dignitaries. Depending on the circumstances, many of these could be addressed either formally or informally.

Touch-typing instruction on manual typewriters with the aim of reaching at least 40 words a minute was essential, as well as shorthand at 100 words a minute using the Pitman's method. It was challenging to acquire these mechanical skills after spending four years learning how to do research, dissect treatises, and "think." It was as though we had to cleanse our brains of all we had acquired at university and develop a different way of absorbing knowledge.

Bookkeeping was compulsory and complicated as we had to learn Double Entry bookkeeping, which was the giving of value by one side and the receipt of that value by the other. Long before a decimal system had been introduced in England, transactions were in pounds, shillings, and pence. With 20 shillings to a pound, and 12 pence (pennies) to a shilling, one's mathematical skills were sorely strained. While working part-time at a café in Hampstead, that brother John had helped me find, I found making change just as difficult as double-entry bookkeeping, especially as mental arithmetic was never my forte. The café, serving coffee and light suppers, had a Spanish flavor with the occasional artist performing and giving instruction in Spanish dancing. I enjoyed getting to know the owners, the Spanish dancer, and the clientele.

As well as waitressing in the Hampstead café, the school arranged for some students to practice their typing and shorthand with transient clients. I took dictation and typed some letters for a man who seemed to have a rather shady business dealing in armaments. In spite of this, I visited him in his upstairs flat to receive and deliver the work. Happily, he always behaved like a gentleman and respected my engagement status.

I did enjoy London life. Pete's brother, Bruce, took me to the theater to see plays or hear concerts, and even though I was engaged, I participated in a few parties organized by the café owners and friends of my brothers. Just before Christmas I took an overnight train to St. Andrews to attend the Sallies ball as Pete's partner. Unfortunately, Pete was not too happy with me as I had a cold, and he thought I was overdoing the socializing in London. We were feeling the strain of being apart. Telephone calls were expensive and difficult as both of us had to use instruments in public hallways, so we wrote letters frequently. To my shock, I discovered that some of my mail had gone astray. Letters from Mummy with money and love letters from Pete had been stolen from the college mailroom by a student. After discovering and reporting the theft, I had all my correspondence mailed to a staff member to pass on safely to me.

The secretarial course finished in March 1956. I was glad it was over. I really wanted to find a job using my newly acquired skills before I forgot them, but Mummy wanted me at home to prepare for our June wedding. As we were to leave for America soon after the ceremony, I couldn't refuse her. Always generous where clothes were concerned, Mummy bought me a trousseau and insisted that her dressmaker create my wedding dress. She helped me find a quiet country hotel on the Yorkshire moors where Pete and I could spend a brief honeymoon weekend after the wedding. The rest of our honeymoon would be our sea voyage to the United States. Showing how old fashioned she was, Mummy expressed surprise when I chose a room with only one bed—at least it was a double one. She was also shocked when I told her that we were going to use protection so we could plan when to have babies. While in London, Pete had arranged for me to visit one of the Greenland Expedition doctors, now in private practice, to fit me with a diaphragm. Because I was not yet married, most doctors would not have offered this service. I had to travel some distance across London to find the office. On the way back, I was able to follow the doctor's suggestion that I practice wearing the contraption while jumping on and off buses to make sure it stayed in place.

After so much freedom at university and in London, I found living at home and apart from Pete for four months restrictive and tedious. In 1950, after 15 years at Kirk Ella House, my parents had made the difficult decision to buy a smaller property in the village of Swanland, where swans really did live on the village pond. Everyone was happy and relieved that the war was finally over, but life had changed radically. There were still shortages of food and materials, and also of manpower. It took time for the factories that had been converted to producing armaments and wartime materials to be re-tooled for their original purposes. The role of women had changed. Many had taken over men's work in the factories, or played supportive roles in the forces. Now men wanted their jobs back, and women were no longer needed or respected. Several of our servants had been enrolled in war work, and it was harder to replace them or afford the higher wages expected for domestic work. The large Georgian mansion at Kirk Ella had become too burdensome for my parents. I had lived there from the age of three to 18 and was just about to go to university when we moved. It was a sad time for all of us.

Southwood, our new house, was modern by Kirk Ella standards. It was situated on a quiet tree-lined street with similar-sized houses all around. Two sets of gates between brick posts opened onto a circular driveway. When I was learning to drive with Daddy as my teacher, I had an unfortunate encounter with one of the posts. As I turned off the road to enter through the gate, I pressed the accelerator too hard and drove the car into the brick post. The impact caused the car's horn to jam, letting all the neighbors know that something problematic had happened.

The house had a pseudo-Tudor look with small-paned windows looking onto the street, and French doors opening from the lounge and sitting room onto a pleasant garden stretching down toward open fields with views of the Humber Estuary on clear days. We still kept hens and needed a fulltime gardener to mow the lawn and look after an abundance of flowers and vegetables, but there was none of the grandeur or magic of the garden at Kirk Ella House. The house had five bedrooms each with its own washbasin, but only one bathroom and separate toilet upstairs and a cloakroom downstairs. The front door opened onto a spacious hall with dining room, study, and lounge facing the garden. There was a two-car garage but Daddy now managed without a chauffeur since his driver had been called up during the war. Nanny, no longer needed in her traditional role, took over most of the cooking with Mummy fixing a meal when Nan had her night out. A daily charwoman took care of the cleaning but Mummy, who was extremely particular, dusted every day and insisted that I keep my room spotless.

Pete visited during the Easter holidays. He was always surprised that I seemed to spend more time chatting or gossiping with Nan in her sitting room off the kitchen than enjoying the company of my mother. Pete stayed on the side lines where plans for our wedding were concerned—it was to be a much grander affair than he would have chosen. Although Mummy was charmed by Pete, she was disappointed that I wasn't going to marry the son of one of her friends and stay close to home. She felt that I was marrying beneath me socially, and of course, was horrified that we were going to leave England to travel to America. We couldn't deny the contrast between our backgrounds. I came from an upper-class professional family and Pete from a lower-middle-class working family. My father was a renowned surgeon, Pete's father was a cipher clerk, encrypting and decrypting messages between the Shell Oil Company ships and the company's offices in London. He earned a steady salary but funds were always tight at the end of the month. Pete's family never owned a car or a telephone. We had two cars and several telephones. I had gone to elite boarding schools, and my university expenses were covered by my parents. Pete depended on scholarships for his tuition and residence and was always short of funds. Despite these differences, we loved each other and had confidence that we would manage our future together. I had moved away from my background and had found common ground with Pete and other friends at St. Andrews. Additionally, Pete had many interesting attributes that my young Yorkshire male friends lacked. Certainly, they would have successful careers, inheriting their father's business or joining the family law firm, and we would have lived close to home, but they were stuffy and dull. Pete was so much more interesting having spent two years on an Arctic Expedition. He was physically and mentally tough, intelligent, and dedicated to his chosen career. Also, he possessed a gentleness that augured well for marriage and fatherhood. For now, we had to play our part in the traditional wedding that my parents wanted to give for their only daughter.

A time-honored English wedding in the 1950s meant that

the men would wear morning suits—striped trousers, cutaway jackets over waistcoats, white shirts, smart ties, and for a finishing touch, gray top hats. Female guests wore stylish dresses or suits—no trousers in those days—with hats and gloves. Everyone looked magnificent, but Pete's father refused to attend, saying that there was no way that he was going to get dressed up in a monkey suit. It was disappointing but something that we had to accept. Pete's mother and young 12-year-old sister, Susan, came from London. Mother did her best to make Beatrice Wyllie welcome, but it must have been hard for Pete's mother. Thankfully, Nan helped her and Sue feel more at ease. Pete's brother, Bruce, who was especially handsome—sometimes working as a model—organized, along with a group of Pete's close friends, a suitable bachelor party at a local pub.

My dress was a fitted, cream-colored brocade with long sleeves and a full skirt. The neckline and sleeves were finished with a delicately-beaded collar and cuffs, and I carried a small sprig of flowers flowing down from a white prayer book. A flower coronet and long veil completed my ensemble. My two-best college friends, Mary Auten and Jill Rees, were my bridesmaids. They carried large bouquets of roses and wore long cream dresses with a band of fabric roses bordering a flounced skirt. My page boy was a young cousin in a MacGregor tartan kilt (my father's clan) and ruffled shirt, adding color to the group.

The wedding service was held on June 9, 1956, at All Saints, a small church in North Ferriby, a village within the Humber Estuary. The church, which served the residents of Ferriby and Swanland, was built in 1848. It has a distinctive spire over a square tower with a roofed porch leading to the entry. Pete and Bruce, attired in their finery with top hats on their heads, looked especially handsome as they walked under this porch on their way to the church. My brothers John and Bob and Tony van Toll, a friend of Pete's, were ushers. Disappointingly, my eldest brother George chose not to attend the event. At the time he was estranged from the family but later provided valuable medical advice after our first child was born.

After the ceremony, we all retired to Southwood where, anticipating a cool gray day, a tent had been erected in the garden for the reception with the wedding gifts on display and filling the Jacobean table in the dining room. We had registered our selections of china and crystal at the most prestigious department store in Hull and our guests had been extremely generous. At first it seemed that every gift I opened was another set of crystal

Romy and Pete – wedding photo

glassware: white and red wine, champagne, cocktail, water, and liqueur. But we also received beautiful linens, trays, china, and silverware, both solid silver antique serving pieces and our chosen flatware set. My godfather, who had shared my father's private surgery practice until a disagreement forced them to part ways,

Pete and Bruce arriving at All Saint's Church

had phoned to say he and his wife would like to give us the complete china service that we had chosen. We had decided not to take any of these precious items to America because we would only be there for two years, and it would have been too expensive and burdensome to have everything packed and shipped to Pennsylvania.

A highlight of the reception was using my father's World War I ceremonial sword to cut the three-tier fruit cake, which was decorated with a husky dog on top. After an appropriate amount of time greeting and talking with the guests, Pete and I changed for our brief honeymoon weekend. I wore a new beige-colored suit and small hat with a splendid white fox stole around my shoulders—one of the foxes that Pete had trapped in Greenland and his wedding gift to me.

We spent three nights at the Mallyan Spout Hotel in the village of Goathland, part of the North Yorkshire Moors National Park, and near the seaside town of Whitby. The hotel is a 19th century country house with views over the Esk valley and a short walk from a waterfall of the same name. After enjoying dinner in the hotel dining room, we sat around in the lounge as long as we could, aware that other guests would notice us retiring early and guess that we were newlyweds. We needn't have worried because our photo and wedding had already been reported in the evening newspaper. We were so glad to have time alone. As we got into bed to enjoy some intimacy, I reached for a long cord above the bed thinking that I was turning off the light. Instead it was a bell pull. Soon there was a knock at the door asking if everything was alright. Embarrassed, we assured the maid that we were fine. As we eventually settled down to sleep, there was a big ruckus below our window—which happened to be over the front door. The bar had just closed and the patrons were going home singing and shouting, oblivious of disturbing someone else's rest. Early the next morning, long before we wanted to wake up, there was another loud noise below. This time it was sheep bleating. We were, after all, in the country and sheep were allowed to roam freely around the village.

We spent the next day exploring the countryside, visiting the picturesque harbor of Whitby and the ruins of the town's Gothic Abbey, originally a seventh century Christian monastery. Realizing that we were within easy driving distance of Helmsley, I told Pete that I would like to show him Duncombe Park, the beautiful estate where I had attended Queen Mary's boarding school. We found both Miss Grant and the housekeeper Gladys at home. After brief visits with them, we toured the grounds, allowing me to share many special memories with my new husband.

After returning Mother's car to Swanland, we took the train to St. Andrews where we had rented an apartment on Bell Street for the two weeks before our departure for Pennsylvania State University in America. While Pete finished up his Geology commitments, I was learning how to be a wife, scrubbing the collars of Pete's shirts and washing his clothes in the kitchen sink. I also tried my hand at cooking, proudly serving mashed potatoes and a fresh cauliflower to accompany the main dish. When Pete cut into his vegetable he discovered a large black slug. I was mortified and felt I should have gone to a cookery school instead of a secretarial college. Pete just laughed and said the slug added an interesting spice to the vegetable.

Our stay in St. Andrews went by in a flash and was filled with many tasks for our upcoming move. These included a train trip across Scotland to the US Consulate in Glasgow to get our working visas for the United States. In Glasgow we stayed with cousin Reverend George Blair's daughter, Rosemary Forbes and her husband and children, giving Pete a chance to meet more of my Scottish relatives. Finally, it was time to pack our suitcases and start our journey south, stopping in Edinburgh where my parents came to say goodbye. As I hugged my father at the train station, I had a strong premonition that I would never see him again. We made a brief stop in London to say our farewells to Pete's family. We were excited to begin our American adventure but terribly sad to leave our families. We continued our journey to Southampton where we boarded the *Queen Mary* to sail to America.

The *Queen Mary*, a member of the Cunard-White Star Line, was built by John Brown & Company in Clydebank, Scotland. The 81,000-ton liner sailed primarily on the North Atlantic Ocean from 1936–1967. Like other Cunard liners, it was beautifully furnished, and was powered by several boilers and turbines, all kept in pristine condition in the bowels of the ship. With our limited means, we also traveled in the bowels of the ship. Actually, not quite as deep as the engines, but as third-class passengers we were on the lowest cabin deck. We did have a port hole but the cover had to be closed for most of the voyage due to rough seas. The cabin was as small as they come with two bunks, one on top of the other, a small wash basin, and hardly any room to maneuver—not exactly conducive to honeymoon activity. Moreover, I was dreadfully seasick and spent most of the time either lying on my bunk or sitting on the deck where I could manage to nibble on some dry crackers and drink weak tea. Pete kept superbly fit and enjoyed meals in the dining room. Not many years ago we toured the *Queen Mary*, which was retired in 1967 and moored as a tourist attraction, hotel, and museum in Long Beach, California. Only then did I realize how luxurious it was with its three-story grand salon, two indoor swimming pools, paddle tennis courts, dog kennels, and myriad fancy amenities.

After five rough days at sea, we arrived in New York where my cousin Aileen—my father and her mother were brother and sister—greeted us warmly and drove us to her apartment in Washington, D.C., where our American adventure would begin.

9. PENNSYLVANIA

Pennsylvania State University is a public, land-grant research university with campuses and facilities throughout Pennsylvania.
—Wikipedia

Cousin Aileen drove us back to her apartment in Washington, D.C., where we spent two weeks acclimating to America. I had a hard time adjusting to the air-conditioned interiors and the extremely hot, muggy outdoors of Washington, D.C. Every time we went out I grabbed a cardigan, now to be called a *sweater,* thinking that it would be chilly outside. Aileen was married to Landreth Harrison, an American diplomat who worked for John Foster Dulles, US Secretary of State from 1953–1959. They showed us the famous sights of Washington, D.C., and introduced us to their diplomat friends.

Aileen was fluent in French and German and had led an interesting life. When the Germans took over Paris in 1940, she was a student at Poitiers University, and in early December had been able to renew her studies in Paris. On the morning of December 5, Aileen and many British women of all ages, including some with children, were arrested and taken by train to an old, filthy French barracks, previously occupied by French and British prisoners, at Besançon near the border with Switzerland. Conditions were abominable: inedible food, vermin-infested rooms, straw-sacks for mattresses, and insufficient furniture, dishes, or cutlery. In an account of her experience, Aileen described the kitchens: "the floor was swimming in muddy water. The tables were impregnated with grease and dirt . . . everything was coarse, filthy, repulsive." There were only outside toilets: "a long shed erected over a pit in the ground across which planks were laid at intervals, with no partitions of any sorts." Somehow, the women made improvements themselves, and persuaded the Germans to do likewise. The prisoners organized a school for the children, biweekly variety shows to relieve the boredom, and Catholic and Protestant church services. Eventually, indoor toilets were installed as well as other amenities.

In the spring of 1941, after several months of careful planning and waiting for the mountain snows to melt, Aileen managed to escape. While a friend flirted with the German guard to distract him, Aileen climbed a wall, pushed aside the barbed wire, and took a train to a nearby village. She hid in a barn overnight before tackling a mountain pass. With the help of a French peasant and a good map, she crossed the frontier to Switzerland and was free. She spent the rest of the war in Switzerland, working as an archivist for the British Legation in Berne. She also met her future husband, Landreth, in Switzerland. After the war she held jobs in London, Lebanon, and France where she worked for UNICEF before getting a job in New York with IBM. In 1952 she became John D. Rockefeller III's top woman secretary. In due course, Aileen met up again with Landreth, who forsook his long-term bachelorhood and married her. Because Aileen was a foreigner, the union required the permission of Landreth's boss, John Foster

Dulles. The couple relocated to Washington, D.C., in 1955.

We were anxious to get to Penn State (Pennsylvania State University) located in the small town of State College, where Pete had accepted a research assistantship with Professor Frank Tuttle. Ian Harker, who had just moved from Penn State to the Geophysical Laboratory in Washington, drove us to State College. At first, we stayed in an efficiency apartment consisting of a bedroom-living room combination with a small kitchenette and separate bathroom. It was limiting to say the least. The bed was an uncomfortable sofa bed that had to be unfolded for sleeping. I soon discovered that Pete hadn't forsaken his Greenland habits. Every time he turned over, he took all the bedcovers with him as though he was in a sleeping bag. We also had to decide what kind of toothpaste to share, and my cooking skills, or lack thereof, were again tested when I let the fat catch fire while frying bacon.

Even though I hated to admit it, I felt homesick. We had looked forward to our first visit to America but everything was so different: finding our way around; driving on the other side of the road with our second-hand car, a 1950 Pontiac; shopping for food, medicines, household goods, and clothes; terminology; using a different currency; even how the day was divided with work hours and times of meals being different to British times. I exchanged letters with my parents every week just as I had been made to do in boarding school. Mummy wrote long, warm, chatty letters several pages long on airmail paper. Daddy didn't write every week but when he wrote in his small, typically *doctor* handwriting, his letters were warm and to the point. Without question, I missed the luxury of my home, having someone to do the cooking, cleaning, and shopping. But at least I had experienced living away from home, with 11 years at boarding school and four years at university. We soon established a routine. On a Saturday, when he wasn't fishing in the nearby mountain lakes and streams, Pete helped me shop for groceries and clean the apartment. We found a small greengrocer's shop on our street owned by an Italian, who had difficulty understanding some of our pronunciations: we had to learn to say tomatoes with a long "a" instead of an "ah."

Members of Pete's new department did their best to make us welcome. We bonded with an English couple, Howard and Marie Gillery and their young son, Steven. They were especially helpful because they spoke our language—actually with a Yorkshire accent—understood our home sickness, and helped us learn the differences in food ingredients and how to convert English recipes. I still use Marie's Christmas cake recipe, making it without fail every December. In anticipation of their growing family—they were expecting twins—the Gillerys had bought a townhouse and suggested that we take over their one-bedroom apartment. We were so happy to move to a more spacious unit that we soon called home. The apartment was on the third floor of an old building on Frazier Street, next door to the Fire Station, resulting in frequent disturbances when the fire engine was called to duty. A Judge, who smoked cigars, had an office on the first floor and another American couple lived on the second floor. Not long after we moved in, this kind couple invited us to join them in their custom of watching a TV program shown at 9:00 P.M. one night a week. The second year, a young Indian couple replaced them. The husband had traveled back to India to marry a bride selected by his family. Having recently experienced arriving in a strange country, we did our best to help the wife adjust. We soon got used to the smell of Indian cooking wafting up the stairs to our unit. Years later, when we traveled to India, we met them again in Calcutta.

Our furnished unit consisted of a bedroom, living room, kitchen separated from a small dining area by a half wall and counter, and a bathroom. Although it was vastly different from my childhood home, I was determined to make it as attractive as possible. I bought sheer drapes to cover the venetian blinds on the living room window, painted one wall dark green to pick up one of the colors in the sofa's upholstery, and added a nice bedspread and pillows in the bedroom. I certainly missed having someone to clean and do laundry. We did have access to primitive laundry equipment in a dark, fusty basement where spiders lurked in the corners. There was a washing machine but no dryer; only a temperamental electric ringer which frequently spun around out of control as it squeezed water out of the washing. We used the equipment for our clothes but sent our sheets to a laundry. At least the apartment was adjacent to the main street and shops, and within easy walking distance of campus.

When Pennsylvania authorities decided to establish a state college in 1855, they chose the intersection of two diagonals drawn across a map of the state. Intended originally to be an agricultural college and known as the Farmers High School of Pennsylvania, the college was renamed Pennsylvania State University in 1953. The village of State College soon became a town fully integrated with the university. At an elevation of 1,200 feet above sea level, the town is surrounded by rolling farmland, forests, and a stretch of the Appalachian Mountains, with Nittany Mountain giving its name to the university football team (the Nittany Lions) and lion mascot. During our stay, the town was compact, small, and limited by Pennsylvania's strict liquor regulations to beer only in restaurants and bars. Both the nearest liquor store and hospital were 12 miles away in Bellefonte. Upset by the lack of a liquor store, Pete wrote a letter to the editor of the local newspaper, *The Centre Daily Times*, expressing disappointment that such restrictions existed in the United States. Years later the town now has both liquor stores and its own hospital, and new residential neighborhoods have multiplied on the outskirts.

The university is a land-grant research center with 19 commonwealth campuses and five special mission campuses throughout the state. The main center is University Campus where enrollment now exceeds 46,800 graduate and undergraduate students, making it one of the largest universities in the United States. Accordingly, the campus grounds have doubled in size since our time.

The quality of education is comparable with Ivy League schools, and even before some of the university's scientific research became renowned throughout the world, certain areas were already greatly respected. Under the guidance and supervision of Professor Frank Tuttle, Pete was fortunate to embark on pioneering laboratory experiments that reproduced chemical reactions at temperatures and pressures at considerable depths within the Earth. He explains his work in these words:

Experiments were started at near-surface crustal pressures (down to a depth of 30 km or so), and eventually reaching pressures and temperatures corresponding to mantle depths of about 150 km. The experiments were designed to determine the effects of "gaseous materials" under high pressure (such as water, carbon dioxide, fluorine) on the minerals of the deep rocks that generate the low-density melts that can rise toward the surface of the crust. Some rising deep-seated melts (magmas) become trapped at various depths, and crystallize to form the large solid masses, such as granite or gabbro, often associated with mountain ranges. Other melts are less dense and break through the surface crust forming lavas, volcanic eruptions, and spectacular volcano peaks. The differences in mineralogy and temperature of lavas and near-surface rocks could be correlated with those of experimental results on mineral assemblages ("rocks" with hot gases) formed at specific pressures and temperatures, providing clues about the conditions of initial deep melting, and of crystallizing as they rose through, or as rock masses within, or lavas erupting through to the Earth's surface.

Pete's work with Frank Tuttle was the foundation of a brilliant career. Together with many colleagues and graduate students, he published hundreds of scientific articles. His textbooks, *The Dynamic Earth* (1971) and *The Way the Earth Works* (1976) brought the plate tectonics revolution into the classroom. In addition to the Polar Medal (1954) and the Miller Prize (1955) at St. Andrews, Pete received six medals for his scientific work over the course of his career, including the Mineralogical Society's Roebling Medal. He was also made a fellow of seven international science academies, and was awarded an honorary D.Sc. by St. Andrews.

At the same time as doing research with Tuttle, Pete was writing up his earlier examination of the picritic rocks in Soay, Scotland, that Professor Harald Drever had suggested as a stimulating study for his St. Andrews Ph.D. thesis. The thesis was submitted to St. Andrews for examination by the Ph.D. Committee of Professors

Pete outside Mineral Sciences Building, Penn State, in 2012

appointed from other UK universities. They concluded that the research and its results merited the degree, making my husband Dr. Pete in 1958. Following this, Pete became Assistant Professor of Geochemistry at Penn State.

I, too, found a job and was so pleased to be able to put my secretarial training into practice, but not without some challenges. I obtained a position as Secretary to the Dean of Summer Sessions, a department established specifically to organize the university's extensive summer programs. The offices were located in the College of Humanities bordering the main campus axis. My first shock was being shown how to turn on my typewriter; I had learned typing on a manual machine and had no idea how to manage an electric one. The second shock was discovering that no one else used Pitman's shorthand; Gregg's shorthand was the American standard so if I got stuck over one of my Pitman scribbles, I was on my own. The third shock was finding out that English and American spelling is different and no one could tell me the rules—if such existed. Every letter that I typed had to be retyped until I finally learned American spelling. It was a rough beginning, but all the other young women in the office and adjacent offices went out of their way to be kind and helpful to this interesting foreigner. At least my boss, Dean P. C. Weaver, received many compliments on the charming telephone voice and accent of his new English secretary.

As well as learning American spelling, we had to adjust our vocabulary, again without any rules to which we could refer. We had an especially hard time in chemist shops, now to be called drug stores. We wanted to buy some *face flannels* and had to mimic washing our faces with something before we found the

Romy as secretary to Dean of Summer Sessions, Penn State

word *wash cloth*. We learned that *cotton wool* was just *cotton* and that there was no such thing as the English staple disinfectant *Dettol*—I still have a bottle in our medicine cupboard I brought back from England years ago. *Full stops* were *periods*; *rubbers* were not prophylactics but *erasers*; *lorries* were *trucks*; and *petrol* was *gas*. It was also an eye opener to comprehend the vastness of the United States, and that many inhabitants of a small rural Pennsylvania town like State College had never traveled out of their state, or even flown in an airplane. We were surprised when one of my office companions asked, "You mean they don't use dollars in England?"

Pete was excited to be part of Tuttle's research group, and we made new friends quickly, filling our social calendar with a variety of activities. In spite of being a novice chef, we dared to invite a few friends over for dinner. I remember one occasion when, thinking that I had turned on the oven, I discovered that the gas was on but not lit. Just as our guests were walking up the stairs, I threw a match into the oven, resulting in a loud bang as the gas lit. Another time, I had been using a hand beater to whip up a dessert mix and left the beater in the bowl which fell over, spilling the contents onto the floor. I confess to scooping up the mix and putting it into the pie shell regardless. A more successful meal was cooking a lamb roast for Jim and Carolyn Curtis—Carolyn was called Squeaky by her close friends—who proclaimed it the best piece of beef they had tasted in a long time. I then explained that it was roasted lamb—meat that Squeaky would never have chosen to eat.

The Division of Earth Sciences organized potluck picnics at Black Moshannon, a state park covering nearly 3,500-acres of forests and wetlands with a large lake for swimming and boating. The park had many trails, rare plants, and animals, and was especially good for bird watching. Another popular destination for weekend recreation was the 256-acre Whipple Dam State Park, which also had a lake and hiking trails. We soon adjusted to barbeques with hot dogs and hamburgers and all the trimmings, and I learned to make salads or bean casseroles for our contribution. Other outings included driving up to Sky Top, a geologically interesting and well-known view point on Bald Eagle Mountain just west of State College. Interstate 99 from Altoona cuts through Sky Top and reminds a traveler that the area is famous for its rock, which is ideal for quarrying, as well as providing an uninterrupted view of Happy Valley, as the area is frequently called.

In addition to mountain outings, we often congregated at someone's house or apartment for a party. Just as Mike Banks wrote, Pete was capable of "going to town with unrivalled exuberance." He was quite adept at drinking plenty of beer, but was always fun and able to sober up when it was time to go home.

Our new friends became life-long friends. Most of the husbands were colleagues of Pete's in the Division of Earth Sciences: Len and Lisa Herzog were wonderful hosts, often holding parties at their home. When we arrived at Penn State, Len was on the faculty and then left to set up his own company, Nuclide Corporation, which manufactured mass spectrometers, quickly growing from a one-room laboratory to a three-building venture. Like us, Bob and Martha Clayton were newly married. They eventually divorced and had other partners, but Martha remained one of our dearest friends. Faculty members Ben Howell and Mac Keith were Penn State stalwarts and made us feel especially welcome. Their wives, Connie Howell and Mary Em Keith, were good at "mothering" newcomers and delivering casseroles when the occasion warranted. The Tuttles, Frank and Dawn, were, of course, our guardians and made sure that all members of the division were happy in their work and play.

Our closest friends were Bob and Lois Fudali—Lois became godmother to one of our children and her first child was called Peter. Bob was a devout fisherman, and he and Pete spent many happy Saturdays or Sundays fly fishing in the mountain streams while Lois and I met to chat or sew. Lois was surprised that I didn't know how to use a sewing machine. She felt that any good wife should be able to make and mend clothes. Lois discovered that sewing classes were taught in the town and encouraged me to take one. Eventually, I signed up for several and learned to make my own clothes, even managing to make a tailored suit. Mummy had set me up with a generous trousseau and expected that Pete would give me a dress allowance. But such an extravagance was not in our budget, so making my own clothes was an asset. After I typed his Ph.D. thesis, Pete had bought me a Singer sewing machine to help me with my new hobby.

Additionally, several of my co-workers and their husbands took us under their wing and enjoyed helping their new foreign friends, who had strange accents and terminology, adjust to the American way of life. We were especially indebted to Jim and Squeaky Curtis, Bill and Rose Pethick, and Glenn and Madeline Baughman. Madeline was my office partner and took care of the summer session finances. Squeaky and Rose worked in other offices in the same building. Some of the couples lived in trailers where we joined them for barbeques and beer parties. Most of the husbands of my work compatriots were graduate students or post-docs in engineering and other divisions, and all of our new friends were enthusiastic football fans.

Football is an essential part of Penn State life. From 1892 to 1992 the Penn State Nittany Lions was an independent team and from 1950–1965 it was coached by Rip Engle who never had a losing season, although his final season was a 5–5 tie. In 1966, Joe Paterno took over from Engle. Paterno coached both as an assistant and then head for 62 years, the longest of any coach at any school. In 1993, during Paterno's tenure, the team joined the NCAA/Football Bowl Subdivision as a member of the Big Ten Conference. They have always had an impressive record of wins, including many successes at the Orange Bowl, the Fiesta Bowl, the Sugar Bowl, and the Rose Bowl. Penn State's Beaver Stadium has been expanded and improved several times and is now the second-largest stadium in the western hemisphere. Soon after our arrival, Frank Tuttle took us to a game, but we had a hard time understanding it and found it boring. The men seemed to spend all the time on the ground, not unlike British rugby scrums, which had been nearly fatal for Pete. We did enjoy the half-time entertainment with attractive cheerleaders and marching bands, but we never became football fans.

In our spare time we enjoyed various forms of exercise. We both played tennis, Pete with a group of men, and I with compatible women for singles or doubles. Sometimes we played together. Pete hit the ball well, but his play was uneven and his frequent errors annoyed me. I agreed with his brother Bruce that Pete was like an elephant on the tennis court. His broad frame was more suited to rugby football and boxing which had been his strengths until he broke his neck. We did, however, enjoy golf, usually playing a two-ball foursome with the Fudalis until we were told by other players that it was not an acceptable method. I was also told off for wearing shorts that were too short—shorter than the customary Bermuda shorts worn for golfing. Additionally, Pete played squash with some of his geology colleagues and occasionally with Joe Paterno, the football coach.

Like many small towns, State College put on a big show for the July 4 Independence Day celebration. Several local bands with properly attired baton twirlers, boy scouts, floats either on open truck beds or decorated cars, and assorted riders on horseback marched down College Avenue followed by a grand firework display in the evening. It was fun to watch and helped us understand the American traditions.

In September of 1956, not long after our arrival at Penn State, we were invited to a wedding in Philadelphia by Judi Pennock, a friend of ours at St. Andrews who had spent the 1954–55 academic year away from Sweet Briar College in Virginia, as an exchange student in Scotland. She was also one of my American friends on the ski trip to Austria. Judi's family were Quakers and the wedding followed the Quaker practice: there is no officiant and no one giving away the bride. A wedding certificate is signed after the couple exchange their promises. They were not vows because Quakers intend to tell the truth at all times. Everyone sat silently in the Friends meeting house until Judi and Al Lilley felt moved to stand up and state their promises. After that other members stood up and spoke a few words. The meeting was followed by a more traditional reception in a garden. Judi looked beautiful in a simple dress, sleeveless with a fitted bodice and long full skirt, and Al wore a dark suit. Although the ceremony seemed strange to us, the Pennocks made us feel very welcome, inviting us to spend our first Christmas in America with them. I stayed in touch with Judi's mother until she died, and we still exchange holiday newsletters with Judi.

Soon after our arrival in State College, we had bought a second-hand car, a well-used 1950 Pontiac, which frequently gave us trouble, including a blow-out on the Pennsylvania turnpike. It also overheated every time we drove up steep inclines. However, in spite of many repairs, the car transported us on interesting explorations of our new country.

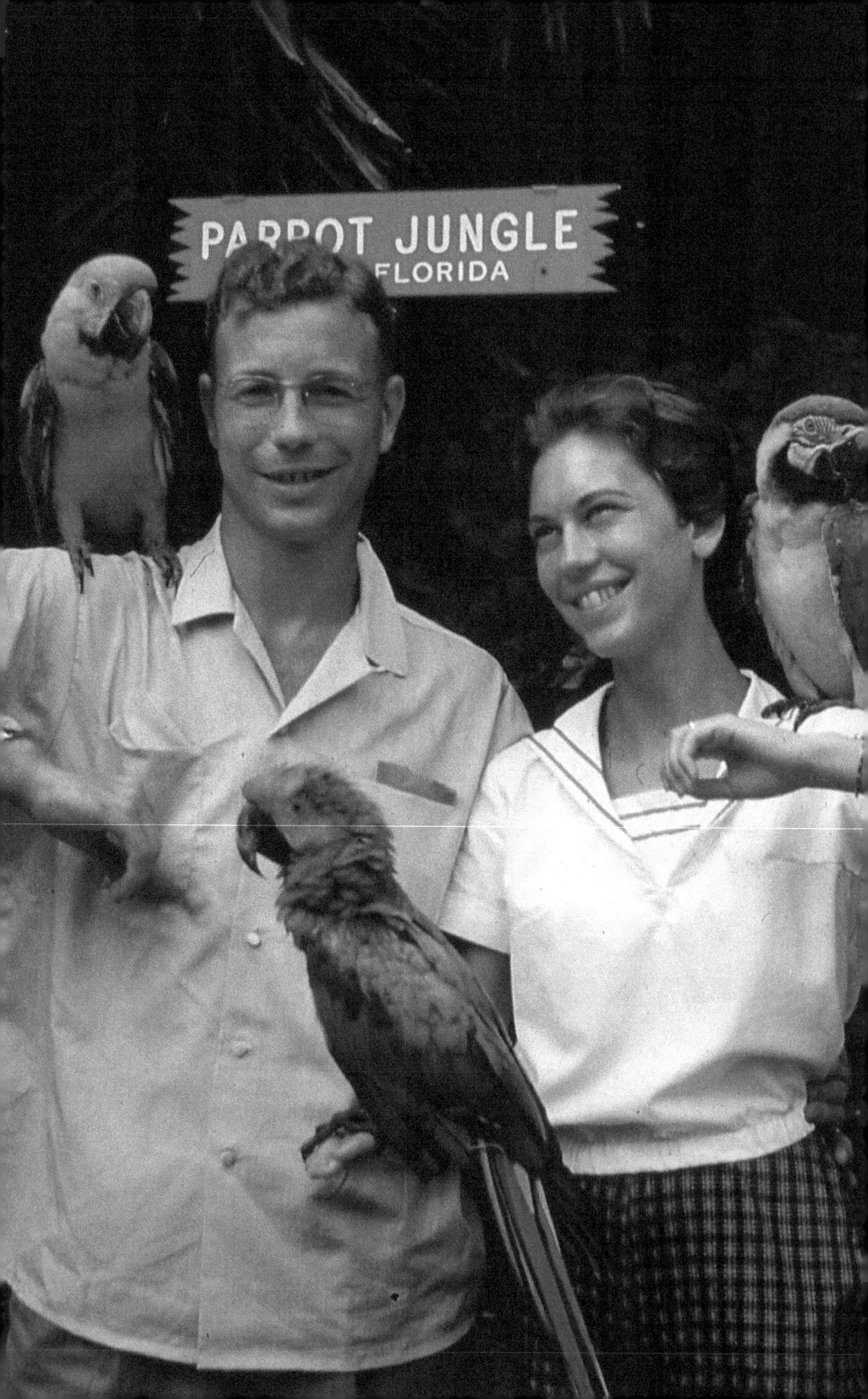
PARROT JUNGLE
FLORIDA

10. EAST AND SOUTH

Oh, beautiful for spacious skies,
For amber waves of grain,
For purple mountain majesties
Above the fruited plain!
—"America the Beautiful" by Katherine Lee Bates

During our three-year sojourn at Penn State—initially our expectation was to stay for two years but we were persuaded to extend our visit for another year—we took two long road trips to learn the history and explore the countryside of the United States. We felt this was our only chance because we didn't expect to come back again. Pete was on a Fulbright Travel Grant that required him to return to England after three years. Moreover, we planned to live and work in Great Britain, because we had no intention of being part of the mid-20th century brain drain when many highly-qualified Brits emigrated to other countries.

We had already visited my cousins in Washington, D.C., several times, attended a wedding in Philadelphia, and even ventured as far north as Niagara Falls. But at the end of our second year, 1957, we embarked on a much more extensive tour taking us

Pete & Romy at the Parrot Jungle, South Miami, Florida

to the east coast and south to Florida. We left State College on September 21 and returned on October 13, having driven nearly 4,000 miles in four weeks. I kept a diary and after our return I typed a long seven-page letter to my parents with details of all the places that we visited. At the beginning of the letter I wrote:

> We had a most marvelous vacation—every minute of it and every place we saw was a great experience. I think the most wonderful part was being together and seeing and experiencing everything together and just being with each other all day. We have never spent so much time together and we were both so relaxed and happy. It was Pete's first vacation since before the war so he really appreciated it and it was so good for him to get away from his work, and he was so gay and relaxed. . . . We loved Florida . . . but I don't think I would like to live there, it would be strange to have the same climate all the year round, and it gets very hot in June, July, and August. . . . Pete looked so like an American tourist with his shorts and sports shirts and two cameras slung round his neck—it was priceless.

In my diary, I also recorded our mileage and all our expenses. We took turns driving our Pontiac, which held up surprisingly well. One day, when I was driving a wasp stung me. Although I was in pain, I managed to stop the car without swerving, and Pete pulled the stinger out. We especially enjoyed learning some of the history of America and seeing the changing landscape so new and different to us. After stopping where the Battle of Gettysburg was fought, we spent the night on the outskirts of Washington, D.C., with the sister of Ann Waterman, the American exchange student who had arranged for us to sit together on the skiing outing to the Cairngorms in Scotland. From D.C., we drove down Route 1 to Fredericksburg to visit the historic town of Williamsburg, Virginia. Williamsburg, which forms a "Historic Triangle" with Jamestown and Yorktown, had been the capital of the Virginia Colony from 1699 to 1780, and had played an important role in the American Revolution, about which we knew little—American history had not been part of my syllabus at St. Andrews, and what we knew was only the British side. Although it was old by American standards, it didn't seem that old to us having been accustomed to the medieval ruins surrounding our university. The old part of Williamsburg has been completely restored to its original plan with some streets too narrow for vehicular traffic. All the tour guides and people working in restaurants and taverns were dressed in colonial costumes. Our visit focused on the historic district where we toured the Governor's Palace, the official residence of the British Governors of the Colony of Virginia before the revolution. We also walked around the campus of the College of William and Mary, founded in 1693 by England's King William III and Queen Mary II, the second-oldest institution of higher education in the United States—a neophyte by St. Andrew's standards. After resisting the temptation to buy a souvenir at a craft shop, we had dinner at the famous neo-classic-designed Williamsburg Inn built in 1937 by John D. Rockefeller, Jr., leaving us with a memory that became especially significant later in our trip.

The next day, on our way from Virginia to North Carolina, we crossed the James River, which begins in the Appalachian Mountains and reaches the ocean at Chesapeake Bay. We stopped for the night in Smithfield where our motel cost $6, which was typical of most overnight stays, except Williamsburg where we had to pay $9; meals ranged from $2 for breakfast to $5 and occasionally $9 for supper—so cheap by today's standards.

From Smithfield we drove through South Carolina and Georgia, "very marshy and swampy country all flat and uninteresting," as well as miles upon miles of agricultural and wooded scenery. By our fifth day we reached St. Augustine on the northeast coast of Florida. St. Augustine is regarded as the oldest city in the U.S., having been founded in 1565 by the Spanish and featuring Spanish colonial architecture. Here we toured the city's oldest house with a beautiful garden and Spanish moss hanging languorously from the trees. We also visited the 17th century Castillo de San Marco, the oldest masonry fort in the continental United States. The name of the fort has changed many times depending on which country was governing Florida: under Spanish rule it was always Castillo de San Marco; under British rule it became Fort St. Mark; and when it joined the Union in 1845, the citadel became an army base named Fort Marion until an Act of Congress in 1942 restored its original Spanish name.

After absorbing some of the history of St. Augustine, we arrived at Marine Land just in time for the main attraction, the porpoise school and feeding. We were amused by the tricks, with balls and rings, that the porpoises performed. One poor porpoise, dressed in a skirt, rode around the pool on a surfboard. From below, we were able to see the tanks of fish, including large sharks, and watch an employee in a diving suit feeding the fish.

We then drove on to Daytona Beach where we found a motel right on the ocean with a pool. I was impressed with the nicely furnished room and its two double beds. Before going out to supper, we had a swim in the pool. As we were getting dressed, I discovered to my horror that I had mislaid my engagement ring. Because it was an antique and one of the stones had fallen out but been found and reset in London, I didn't wear it all the time. After searching through all my clothes and luggage, I thought hard and remembered that I had taken it off and laid it on a shelf when I washed my hands in the Ladies' Room at the Williamsburg Inn— four days ago. Immediately, we wrote to them describing the ring and what had happened, but never expected to see it again. I tried to put aside the disappointment. Nevertheless, the loss hung over our trip like a recurring bad dream.

We now drove inland, stopping on the way to enjoy wonderfully fresh orange juice, to Silver Springs, a group of artesian springs that has been a tourist attraction since before the Civil War. In the 1920s, the land around the springs was developed and the area became the Silver Springs Nature Theme Park featuring animal exhibits, amusement rides, and glass-bottom boat tours. We took the boat tour and were captivated by the translucency of the water and the beauty of the springs. We also visited Ross Allen Reptiles where we saw displays of tortoises and alligators, and a man milking the venom from snakes. In addition, there were flocks of pink flamingos strutting about and pecking the dirt, peacocks displaying their multi-colored fan feathers, noisy and brightly colored parrots, and a Seminole Indian village where women were making intricate baskets. When we left at 5:30 P.M. to drive to Cypress Gardens it was too dark to climb the Citrus Tower, a monument to Central Florida's citrus industry, but we did admire the acres and acres of orange groves.

Our destination was Fort Lauderdale, via Lake Wales, Lake Okeechobee, and West Palm Beach to stay with Jim and Carolyn

Curtis. Carolyn was one of my best friends who worked in the Humanities Building at Penn State. She had the unfortunate nickname of Squeaky. I called her that for many years until she persuaded her friends to use her real name. Jim had been a graduate student in Engineering at Penn State, had graduated at the end of our first year, and now had a position with a construction company in Florida. They had kindly invited us to stay with them so we could experience Florida to the fullest.

On our way we stopped at Cypress Gardens, a botanical garden and theme park near Winter Haven, to see the renowned waterski show. We were stunned by the skills of the skiers, dressed in colorful costumes, forming different patterns with banners spelling out CYPRESS GARDENS as they sped over the water. I told my parents that "we sat in a special photographers' gallery with our cameras, and someone told us just the right exposure to use and the precise moment we should take the picture to get the best result. It was quite amusing and also very helpful."

Our next stop was the Bok Mountain Lake Sanctuary and Singing Tower, a contemplative garden and bird reserve designed by the renowned landscape architect Frederick Law Olmsted, Jr., just north of Lakes Wales. Over a hundred bird species, including wild turkeys and sandhill cranes, find refuge at the sanctuary. The Gothic Revival and Art Deco tower built on Iron Mountain, one of the highest points in Florida, is 205 feet tall with 60 carillon bells that ring out across the tranquil gardens and create a sense of serenity conducive to contemplation.

Our nine days with Jim and Squeaky were full of sightseeing, sometimes with them and sometimes on our own, or just with Squeaky because Jim had to work. It was so generous of them to put us up for such a long visit. They lived in an apartment, which was more like a semi-detached cottage. The front and back doors opened onto a garden with trees and an umbrella providing shade for sitting. Our friends gave us their bedroom, and they slept in the living room because Jim had to get up early for work. I wrote Mummy and Daddy that the Florida weather was perfect—averaging 86 degrees and the same in the water. For several days, we enjoyed acquiring a tan on the beach and swimming in the ocean. It was a unique experience for us Brits. We had a hard time believing the warmth of the sea, vastly different from the 50-degree ocean in St. Andrews. Nor had we ever experienced such beaches with broad expanses of golden sand instead of little patches of sand between rocks and pebbles on England's northeast coast. I told my parents that we were very careful to lather ourselves with suntan lotion and only sunbathe for a short time each day until we had gotten a tan and become used to the sun. When we returned to State College everyone envied our tans. We also shopped for more tropical clothes: bathing suits, shorts, hats, and sunglasses at Sears & Roebuck. Always a sucker for expensive clothes, I managed to find a wonderful dress on sale at a boutique. It was white silk with vertical and horizontal bands of black. I called it my Piet Mondrian dress and enjoyed wearing it many times. Pete bought a mask, flippers, and snorkel, and we both used the equipment to snorkel and view colorful fish—another new experience. In my letter I wrote:

> We found a place where there was a coral reef running out and Pete proceeded to practice skin diving. I tried some too and realized how beautiful the scenery is under water. I didn't find it too difficult swimming

Romy on the beach, Fort Lauderdale, Florida

underwater but I had difficulty keeping my bottom under. Pete would laugh so much because I would dive under and in no time my bottom would be floating near the top again.

For my parents, I described the Florida scenery and houses—so unlike anything in England:

It is a tropical climate and is warm all the year around, everywhere there are palm trees and cypress trees, beautiful flowers, hedges of hibiscus, alligators, snakes etc. and some stuff called Spanish moss which hangs on the branches of certain trees. It is not a parasite but feeds on the moisture in the air. Everything and everywhere is damp and anywhere where the land had not been drained are swamps. The houses are quite lovely, the architectural styles are either the old Spanish type of house with an oddly tiled roof and arches and little windows cut in white walls, or very modern ranch style of house, essentially American and particular to Florida and probably California. You hardly ever see two-story houses, just the apartment buildings which are air conditioned. There are no basements as the town is only about 7 feet above sea level. The houses are all very new and modern and painted in the most beautiful shades of pale blue, pink, green, and yellow. When people go away for any length of time they close their houses and put silver-looking shutters over the windows to keep out the rain and bugs (in abundance). Fort Lauderdale is a spotlessly clean town and very new having only been developed in the last 10 years.

I told them about a new part of Fort Lauderdale under development where swamps were being drained and canals made so all the houses had their own waterfronts accessing about 125 miles of navigable waterways. I also described several Seminole Indian reservations with no road access and residents living in thatched-roof huts open on all sides. The Indians made their living by raising cattle, fishing, and fabricating souvenirs.

In addition to enjoying the beach, we toured the areas in the vicinity of Fort Lauderdale. These included driving out to Key West, the southernmost point of the United States and part of the Florida Keys archipelago, a chain of islands linked by causeways. We were struck with the antiquity of Key West with its pastel-colored houses surrounded by tall palms against a vast backdrop of turquoise-colored ocean. Another day we drove to Miami to see the Hialeah Race Track Park which has the largest flock of Flamingos filling the infield lake area of the racetrack. The birds were imported from Cuba in 1934 by Joseph Widener, and Hialeah is the only place where they have successfully reproduced in captivity. They certainly created a unique image. As they clustered together their bodies looked like a vast pink carpet with long necks and heads forming rods wavering above the horizontal mass. Driving through Miami on our way back, we admired the many luxurious hotels with their exotic entrances and wondered if we would ever stay in such places.

Fort Lauderdale is regarded as a gateway to the Everglades, so a jungle cruise was a must. After passing expensive and beautiful homes, we entered the Everglades and enjoyed the shade of trees with low overhanging branches, and the sight of many species of exotic flora, fauna, and large alligators. At one stop we visited a Seminole Indian village and witnessed an Indian wrestling an alligator. It was impressive, but we vowed never to go near an alligator. We saw more alligators when we visited the Parrot Jungle in

South Miami. After watching the birds perform tricks, including responding to their names, we were photographed holding some of the colorful and raucous birds.

One day we went to the Bahia Mar Marina and chartered a boat to go deep-sea fishing. With the skipper and one other man, we set out for an afternoon of fishing. After catching some bait, the skipper patroled back and forth between two buoys over what was supposed to be an active fish area, but we had no bites. Suddenly, Pete felt his line catch on something and started to reel it in, pulling hard on the line and turning the handle as he leaned back in his chair with the effort. At this point, we noticed that another boat, some distance away, was coming closer with each exertion that Pete made. The skipper saw it, too, and gave us the cruel news that Pete's line had got caught in a line from the other craft and what he was hauling in was the nearby boat—not exactly the large fish that we had hoped to catch. To add to our disappointment the sky was looking ominously dark and it was beginning to rain, along with loud claps of thunder and flashes of lightning. Quickly, the skipper turned the boat around to head for the harbor. By now it was so dark that he had to use a compass to find the way. A very wet and bedraggled pair of tourists headed back to the Curtis's apartment to change and go out to Miami Beach to see a showing of *Around the World in Eighty Days* on a Todd-AO screen, a high-resolution widescreen format, developed in the mid-1950s by Mike Todd, United Artists Theaters, and the American Optical Company.

A more successful venture onto the ocean was a moonlight cruise with Jim and Squeaky to the Barefoot Mailman, a motel between the sea and the inland canal north of Pompano Beach named for the first U.S. mail carriers who, because there were no roads, had to walk and travel by boat between Palm Beach, Lake Worth, Miami, and other towns to the south. We enjoyed an excellent dinner and entertaining floor show. Wherever we went on an organized tour, in the Everglades or to the Barefoot Mailman, our skipper would talk about the houses that we passed, sometimes telling us who owned them and how much they cost.

After enjoying the hospitality of our friends and experiencing many memorable adventures in South Florida, it came time to leave and head home. From Fort Myers, we drove up the west coast of Florida through Sarasota and over the Sunshine Skyway to St. Petersburg, staying at a motel on Treasure Island Beach. The next morning, we stocked up on Florida fruit—40 pounds of oranges and 20 pounds of grapefruit—and drove to Clearwater through Tarpon Springs, which boasts having the largest sponge industry in the world, past Weeki Wachee Springs State Park and up Route 19, spanning the Suwannee River three times. Finally, we crossed the Florida border, stopping for the night at Hawkinsville the "Harness Horse Capital" of Georgia. On October 9, 1957, the 19th day of our trip, we drove from Hawkinsville to Cherokee, North Carolina. Once we had passed the University of Georgia in Athens, we began to enter beautiful mountain scenery. We had planned our trip well because it was now time for the leaves to change color. After stopping in Clayton to get a new water pump for the car and souvenirs in Cherokee Village, we drove up a winding road to the top of the Great Smoky Mountains National Park, which has some of the highest peaks in the eastern United States. From the top we enjoyed the sprawling views of valleys and hills clothed in their autumnal hues. We learned that the park straddles the ridgeline of the Great Smoky Mountains, part of the Blue Ridge Mountains, a division of the Appalachian Mountain chain. Although the scenery was exceptionally beautiful, we were disappointed not to meet any bears. After supper at a French restaurant we went to Homespun Valley Mountaineer Village, viewed a collection of hillbilly memorabilia, and listened to mountain music, strange to us but typically American.

Day 21 took us from Gatlinburg, Tennessee, on to Charlottesville, Virginia, where we stayed with Judi and Al Lilley, whose Quaker wedding we had attended the previous year in Philadelphia. The next morning, we toured the University of Virginia where Al was studying law. We were impressed by the beauty of the original campus known for its unified plan of colonial-style buildings. The university was founded and designed in 1819 by Thomas Jefferson, the third president of the United States and author of the Declaration of Independence. From there we drove to see Jefferson's Monticello residence, plantation, and display of his inventions. We admired the Palladian-style neoclassic architecture of the main house, and the extensive grounds leading to tobacco fields and mixed crops—all set on the top of a small mountain with spectacular views of the Blue Ridge Mountains. In the late afternoon we drove along the Skyline Drive, admiring the scenery and fall colors of greens, golds, russets, and pale yellow. On Day 23, after a night at another $6 motel in Winchester, Virginia, and a purchase of Virginia apples, we took Route 522 to Hancock, Pennsylvania, and home.

The next day we collected our mail and found a small, padded envelope from the Williamsburg Inn. Inside, to our total surprise was my engagement ring—an unexpected and perfect end to an adventurous vacation. We felt so grateful for the honesty of some stranger who had found the ring and handed it over to the management.

11. THE WILD WEST

The Wild West was so named for the lawlessness of the untamed territories west of the Mississippi River—the western United States during its frontier period—1865–1895.
—Kelly La Rue in Quora

Our second trip was a Wild West Adventure—a 37-day driving and camping holiday, taking a northern route across the United States from Pennsylvania to California, and a southern route back. We drove nearly 8,800 miles, averaging about 300 miles a day, and staying in camp sites with occasional stops in motels to shower and recoup. Again, I kept a diary and recorded all our stops, our mileage, and our expenses. Although I had lists of all our provisions, the diary doesn't record whether we used one large map book, separate maps for each state, or AAA Trip Ticks. I did note that occasionally we bought a local guide book, and undoubtedly Pete made sure we had a good travel plan with detailed directions. The purpose of the trip was two-fold: firstly, instead of visiting popular tourist sites and enjoying the beaches and ocean in Florida, we wanted to experience the vastness and variety of the American midwest and west; secondly, we decided it was time to start our family. If I got pregnant in the summer of 1958, I would give birth in the spring of 1959, a few months before we would be returning to England.

Pete, of course, was able to use his Greenland experience to facilitate our camping plans. I only had my Girl Guide proficiency, and had little knowledge of organizing equipment and provisions. A geology colleague of Pete's loaned us a small tent, and we bought air mattresses, sleeping bags, a camping stove, and other equipment from Sears & Roebuck. To help with the pregnancy plan, we chose sleeping bags that could be zipped together to make one double bag, but there was a problem with the tent—it had a center pole. The night before we left, Pete went to the geology department's workshop and built a wood frame to support a shortened pole and straddle our double sleeping bag. It did mean that we had to crawl into bed very carefully to avoid hitting the frame—like performing a limbo dance.

We set out on July 29, 1958, taking turnpikes through Ohio, Indiana, and Illinois. On the third day we camped at Starving Rock State Park near a river in Illinois. That night it poured with rain and our adjusted tent got soaked. It wasn't until we set up the tent the next night that we discovered the canvas had shrunk and Pete's carefully designed frame no longer worked; all we could do was place the center pole to one side, giving the tent a strange angle. At one camp site, a young boy came up to me and said: "Hey, Missus, your tent's falling down."

AUGUST 1, DAY 4: We arrived in Redfield, Iowa, where we stayed with Mark and Jean Bandy whom we had met at Penn State. Mark Bandy (1900–1963) was a prominent American mining engineer and mineral collector, and he had much to discuss with Pete. The Bandys showed us around their own farm and that of a neighbor. We were overwhelmed by the size of the farms, with acres and acres of corn stretching into the distance as far as the eye could see. We visited the largest gas storage place in the United States. It consisted of a dome of porous sandstone, 2,300 feet deep. Gas was piped up from Texas and other states, then pumped down under the dome for storage, before being pumped up again when needed.

The Bandys allowed us to take a short drive in their Cadillac with power steering and air conditioning—a far cry from our beat-up Pontiac, which had already been giving us trouble and causing us to stop for repairs. Fortunately, our car troubles occurred when we were near a gas station or in a town, and we were diligent at getting oil changes and any other ongoing maintenance at regular intervals. At the Bandys, we also took advantage of being able to do some laundry, take showers, enjoy some excellent meals and good conversation before setting off again on our camping adventure.

As Pete had spent two years enduring extreme conditions in the Arctic, spending four months traveling across icy terrain with a sledge and dog team, and pitching a small two-man tent every night, our nearly six-week western adventure must have seemed like the lap of luxury. I had experienced sleeping under canvas in wet conditions at Girl Guide camp, but only for a week. As a result, I have to admit the camping was challenging. Most of the time we spent one night at a campsite so we were constantly pitching the tent and unpacking our provisions, then getting up at 7:00 A.M. to have breakfast, strike camp and be on our way by 8:30 A.M. Although the scenery was often spectacular, only a few places had flush toilets and showers—most of the camp sites were primitive with smelly outhouses full of spiders, and pumps for water—and using the outhouse or toilet in the dark was tricky because of the possibility of bears. In Yellowstone, if I had to go to the toilet in the middle of the night, I made Pete go with me. The hardest part was washing. We could brush our teeth and wash hands and face in a bowl of cold water on the camp table, but anything more private had to be done squatting in the tent with a bucket of cold water. Although the camping was rough, I had had the experience of boarding school and conditions that were vastly different from my luxurious home and upbringing. This trip was an adventure that I could share with my husband who had undergone truly tough living conditions.

On our fifth day we drove through Sioux City at the corner of three states: Iowa, Nebraska, and South Dakota. We had already crossed two time zones and the temperature was climbing into the 90s. The next day we drove to Sioux Falls and across South Dakota past Cheyenne and Sioux Indian reservations. In my diary I described the landscape: "miles and miles of flat, open prairie, sometimes undulating and sometimes just flat." We crossed the wide and beautiful Missouri River, driving through Kadoka to the Badlands in South Dakota. Here we were impressed by: "great ridges and mountains of sandstone made by streams and erosion in the arid atmosphere, with strata of variegated red, brown, and yellow sandstone, some very high forming pinnacles, towers, and turrets."

After camping in the Badlands, we drove across the border into the Black Hills of South Dakota where we visited the famous Mt. Rushmore memorial consisting of 60-foot-high figures of four U.S. Presidents: Washington, Lincoln, Jefferson, and Roosevelt carved at the top of the granite mountain. Our route took us through Custer State Park, and with our car struggling and boiling, we climbed through the high pointed rocks of Needles Highway, and the old mining towns of Deadwood and Lead, famous for the 1876 gold rush and characters like Calamity Jane. The towns were spread over the hillside, and gold was still being mined. It was dark by the time we reached a campsite near the Devils Tower. The tower, which we first viewed as a silhouette against the night sky, looked like the remnant of an old volcano. In the morning we were able to see the spectacular phenomenon, also known as Bear Lodge Butte, more clearly. Pete was especially intrigued by it; he explained that a butte is a small hill with very steep sides and a flat top, rising suddenly above the surrounding plain. In daylight I could appreciate the description provided for tourists: a giant petrified tree stump rising 1,267 feet above the Belle Fourche River Valley. On the way down from our hike to the Tower, we saw a town of prairie dogs, which are like ground squirrels. We found their behavior curious and amusing. They live in burrows, woof like dogs, and have a sentry on duty who sits up and barks at any sign of danger, warning the others who then race down their holes.

A scenic drive through the Big Horn Mountains in Wyoming with views of the valley below was breathtaking but made me extremely nervous. We found a beautiful campsite among the pine trees. The next day we drove over the 8,950-foot-high Granite Pass, enjoying views of mountain peaks covered in dark green pine trees, and a deep canyon formed by the river with brightly colored sedimentary rocks on either side.

On our ninth day, we entered the famous Yellowstone

National Park, the first National Park in the U.S., where we spent four nights—such bliss. Yellowstone Lake is centered over a caldera, which is a dormant volcano feeding many geysers and hydrothermal features. We set up camp in one of the numerous loops of the main campsite and enjoyed the luxury of flush toilets and showers—I was able to wash my hair—a well-stocked store, and plenty of trees for hanging washing lines and food containers with clamped lids out of reach of bears. Bison were occasionally sighted and there were bears aplenty—I kept count and reached 49 bears by the time we left. Every night we went to sleep with a pan and ladle in the tent so we could make a loud noise to scare away animal intruders. One bear encounter proved quite dangerous. From our place in the line of cars pulled off to the roadside—we were being typical tourists—Pete stepped out to take a movie, and I was holding a still camera to record a mother and her cubs, when the mother lunged at Pete. Fortunately, another visitor in the car line saw what was happening and frightened the bear away just in time.

Pete's father introduced him to fishing in London's River Thames when he was a young boy, and it was a pastime that he especially enjoyed. Our campsite in Yellowstone was near the Fishing Bridge so Pete took advantage of it and brought home some delicious fish for supper—a special treat after many meals of canned beans and spam. We also rented a boat to fish on the lake alternating between a spinner, dry and wet flies, and worms. This was the first time I had tried fishing. I thought it was boring and rather pitiful to catch the poor dumb fish, but I was rewarded with a 12-inch trout that I caught with a wet fly.

Most of all we looked in wonderment at the great Yellowstone geysers and bubbling mud. Some areas had vivid colors with appropriate names such as Emerald Pool, Morning Glory, Fountain Paint Pot, and Rainbow Pool. The Old Faithful geyser performed well, rising high above the surface with a great whoosh of steam. We also explored Tower Falls and Mammoth Hot Springs and its famous Terraces, formed by the flowing waters sculpting large travertine limestone terraces as the water drips over the edges from one to another.

Romy with 12" trout caught at Yellowstone

On our way down to Norris Springs, we passed beautiful lakes and Obsidian Cliff, made of rhyolite lava that had cooled so quickly that it didn't have time to crystallize. As a result, it was quenched to a black glass that can be chipped to an exceptionally thin edge.

AUGUST 10, DAY 13: We said goodbye to the camping friends we had made while in Yellowstone, and entered the Grand Teton National Forest, which I described in my diary: "Scenery spectacular—mountains rising sheer from the edge of the lake, very jagged, rocky peaks, many well above the timber line and many old glaciers and quarries to be seen. Drove along the edge of the lake then through meadows with the Teton mountain range always in view." After lunch in Jackson Hole we climbed the 8,431-foot-high Teton Pass. Typically, our radiator boiled just near the top, and it took a long time to get the car going again because of a vapor lock. We took comfort in the fact that other cars boiled. Our destination was Craters of the Moon National Monument in Idaho where we camped. In the morning we admired the volcanic scenery which had been active as recently as 500 years ago. Some scientists believed that the area, with its hollow craters, caves, tree stumps, ropey and jagged lava surface, was similar to the moon—as yet unexplored by man.

We were now well into the glorious scenery of the west. To us it seemed so vast, so endless, with large expanses of space between towns. And the spaces were filled with geological wonders: mountains, forests, lakes, and colorful rocks in unusual formations. When we stopped in towns, we knew that we were in the west because everyone was dressed in blue jeans, cowboy boots, sometimes with spurs, and the ubiquitous large Stetson hats.

As we were on a tight budget, we spent as little as possible on luxuries. We did buy fresh milk, bread or rolls, and occasionally eggs and bacon, but mostly we subsisted on cereals, dried foods, and cans of baked beans, soups, or canned meats. We made regular stops at restaurants for lunch, usually costing less than $2 or $3, and occasionally we stopped for ice cream or dinner. However, to help maintain my sanity, it was essential that we stayed in a motel about once a week. This gave us a chance to take a shower, wash our hair, launder some clothes, and recover from sleeping in a tiny tent with a crazy bar to climb under every night. Stops at the Bandys' farm in Iowa and at their home in New Mexico were especially pleasurable.

Now, after crossing the Snake River, we reached Oregon and had to set our watches to Pacific Standard Time. From a camp in Idlewild State Park near Burns, Oregon, we made our way across miles of flat, sometimes rippling, wilderness covered with scrub and sage and occasional sightings of cattle, until we were rewarded by a view of the Cascade Mountains, another incredible sight. A drive through a dense forest brought us to our destination, Crater Lake. Viewed from the top of the Crater rim, this was the most beautiful lake we had ever seen. The water was deep, clear blue with a tree-covered island in the center surrounded by sheer rock walls. After exploring all sides of the crater, and finding a nice campsite at Rim Village, we hiked down to the lake via a long, windy, steep trail. It took 45 minutes to get down and much longer to climb back up, but we made it. Although it was worth the effort, we decided that the lake was much more beautiful viewed from above. Somehow, the close-up vista lost some of the intensity of the blue color.

AUGUST 14, DAY 17: We reached the California border and were surprised to have our car inspected for fruit, vegetables, plants, or animals. Just before entering Crescent City and our initial glimpse of the ocean, we viewed our first Redwood trees with their massive trunks and spaced-out branches rising high above the ground. We pushed on through lumbering country and deep, dark groves of Redwoods to Garberville. This put us in easy reach of San Francisco, which we planned to enter the next day. I have a note in my diary that I took a shower and ironed some dresses in readiness for our city visit. I took two suitcases on the trip, one with camping clothes: shorts, T-shirts, jeans, slacks, shoes, socks, 12 pairs of panties, bathing suits and wool pajamas; the other case for city visits with a ridiculous number of dresses (five). I described them as: "Italian, red-spotted, pink and mauve, peacock, and green striped." I also packed a cardigan, full petticoat, slips, a panty girdle, dressing gown, two nighties, and two pairs of sandals.

As we drove toward San Francisco, we were immensely impressed with the beauty of the Golden Gate Bridge, the largest single span bridge in the world, set against the backdrop of the city looking like an island with water on three sides. We spent only one night in San Francisco, finding it very chilly, but with much to explore. We were struck with the steep streets where houses have two stories on the front side, and nine in the rear; and the Spanish-style architecture with stucco and adobe houses in pastel colors of pinks, greens, blues, purples, and off-whites, many with wrought-iron balconies and archways. All the shops were colorful with glitzy neon signs, especially in Chinatown, which boasted numerous restaurants, theaters, night clubs, temples, lanterns, and bells blowing in the breeze to keep evil spirits away. We also visited Fisherman's Wharf and enjoyed some fresh shrimps and wondered how any of the yachts could maneuver their way in or out of the packed harbor. After finding a motel near the center, we went "out on the town." I wore my green-striped cotton dress. It had short sleeves, a fitted bodice and waist with a full, three-quarter length skirt gathered from a narrow white band just below the waistline. Even though I had my white cardigan, I remember feeling cold and that my dress was too summery. We took the cable car to Nob Hill and had cocktails and enjoyed the panoramic views from the Top of the Mark lounge of the Mark Hopkins Hotel, the highest building in San Francisco at that time. After a delicious dinner in Chinatown, we went to the Black Hawk nightclub, a well-known club that featured live jazz performances during the period 1949–1963. The night we were there, the Dave Brubeck Quartet performed. In total, the day cost a whopping $40.

Our next significant visit was Yosemite. We drove across the San Joaquin Valley, stopping for the night at Sugar Pine Ranch. A long, winding, narrow, uphill road brought us to the Sierra Mountains, more beautiful redwood trees, and our first view of the glacial gorge of Yosemite National Park. To our surprise the campsite was crowded, and we ended up sharing a space with a friendly, single woman from San Francisco. We drove up the canyon to Happy Isles and down the other side and admired the many waterfalls flowing down the canyon walls, which we learned would flow in full spate in the spring when the winter snows melted. We were in awe of the monster sequoias: some you could walk through and one was large enough to accommodate a car. At the top of Glacier Point we looked down on cars and campsites resembling flies on the green valley floor. In the evening, we watched the Glacier Point Firefall, which had been initiated in 1872 but was stopped in 1968 because it had become too popular and the crowds were ruining the meadow. The display consisted of flaming logs tumbling over the edge of the cliff and down its rocky sides like a glowing waterfall. After a noisy night in the crowded campsite, we spent the next day driving down the mountain, across the San Joaquin Valley again to the coast, then more mountains, apple country with many Latinx people working in the fields, and onto the coastal plateau to Monterey Bay and Carmel. Unfortunately, fog spoiled our views, but we ended the day at a private campsite about two miles south of Big Sur.

AUGUST 18, DAY 21: We skipped Hearst Castle because there was a four-hour wait to get in, and drove on to Santa Barbara. After overcoming our shock at the cost of hotels near the ocean front, we decided to treat ourselves ($12 a night) to one with a swimming pool on Bath Street, just off Cabrillo Boulevard. Eager to try the Pacific Ocean, we changed into bathing suits and went down to the beach only to discover that the water was almost as cold as the North Sea. However, we lay on the beach and enjoyed the warm sun. After dinner at The Town House on State Street, we explored the city center and City Hall and admired the Spanish-Moorish architecture. Day 22 was spent enjoying Santa Barbara. We made use of a foggy morning to take our clothes to a laundromat and write postcards. By the afternoon, the sun had broken through, and the fog drifted away, so we walked to the end of the yacht club pier and found a spot on the sand where I sunbathed and Pete fished from the pier. Many years later, Santa Barbara became one of our favorite places to visit. I have always loved the view from the harbor with the picturesque sight of the yachts, their masts swaying in the breeze, against the backdrop of the town nestled up against the mountains.

Before leaving Santa Barbara, we visited the Mission, one of the Franciscan missions established a day's ride apart along the California coast. We made good time on the dual highway running near the ocean then cutting inland to Los Angeles. Before reaching the city, we stopped at a gas station and bought a map. The attendant was most helpful and pointed out places to see. We learned that Los Angeles is a big sprawling city with many beach communities, a downtown that isn't necessarily the center of the city, active rigs pumping oil from under the city regardless of causing areas to sink, houses built precariously on hillsides, and many distant suburbs with a growing network of freeways. Our route took us through Studio City and Hollywood where we saw some of the motion picture centers; Beverly Hills with its big mansions, luscious gardens, and chauffeur-driven Cadillacs. We managed to find our way to the downtown area with its Civic Center and Olvera Street where the shops and booths retain the spirit of the original Mexican-governed city. Typically, I was tempted to shop, buying a Guatemalan skirt with beautiful gold embroidery, and a tablecloth and napkins. We ended the full day at an air-conditioned $6 motel in San Bernardino, never imagining that one day, Pete's career would bring us to the California Institute of Technology in Pasadena, and a hilltop home with a view across the Los Angeles basin.

AUGUST 21, DAY 24: This was a long, hot drive through the desert to Las Vegas. Even though we took the grades slowly, our car's radiator boiled, and we kept having to stop to throw water on it and wait for it to cool. The scenery seemed so bleak after the forests, lakes, and mountains that we had driven through on our way to California. Here was a wide expanse of nothing but dry sage brush, sand, and hills. In places the sand had blown to the edge of hills, in others, scree and rocks had rolled down from the hills to cover the sand. All the rivers and lakes were dry and there were only a few houses and the occasional gas station. Las Vegas was such a contrast with its opulent hotels and night clubs. We found a reasonably-priced air-conditioned motel and were thankful to get out of the 100-degree heat. In the evening, we went out to dinner and a show which featured the comedian

Joe E. Lewis, and a chorus line with wriggly, sexy dancers naked from the waist up. We observed some of the gambling but didn't participate at the tables. However, I put $1 into a silver dollar machine and won $11 back, and Pete won $8 on a nickel machine.

We began the next morning with a typical western breakfast—steak and eggs for Pete—before driving across more desert to Zion in Utah. There was little vegetation, just bare rock, sandstone, and clay showing striking examples of cross-bedding in the sediments. As we drove deeper into Zion, the rocks, rising high and jagged around us, became more colorful with reds, whites, and mauves among the unusually shaped peaks. Having been discovered by Mormons in 1858, many of the summits had biblical names such Cathedral Mountain, Court of the Patriarchs, and The Temple of Sinawava—the coyote spirit in the Paiute nation. As we admired some riderless horses finding their way back to their stables, our driverless car backed out onto the road, fortunately without doing any damage. We had forgotten to put on the parking break. As the car slid onto the road, there was a slight rise forcing it to stop.

AUGUST 23, DAY 26: took us to the top of Zion canyon, through a mile-long tunnel, before crossing a desert-like plateau with examples of cross-bedding on original sand dunes. After driving through Kaibab National Forest to Jacob Lake, we visited the North Rim of the Grand Canyon, which is known as "the world's most spectacular example of the power of erosion." We looked 5,000 feet straight down into the canyon and were in awe of the red-orange-colored cliffs with their various shapes looking like oriental temples and pyramids. In addition to remains of Indian pueblos, there were five tribes who lived in the region:

Hopi, Navajo, Havasupai, Paiute, and Hualapai. Next, we crossed the Painted Desert, past the Vermilion Cliffs with their beautiful formations and colors of reds, grays, whites, and browns interspersed with patches of green vegetation. As we passed through a Navajo Indian reservation, we observed primitive wooden huts, mud houses, and farms with small crops of corn and a few sheep and cattle—the women especially seemed to retain their original dress and one had a baby on her back in a papoose—to the Grand Canyon Bridge. This is a steel spandrel arch bridge built in 1929 and renamed the Navajo Bridge in 1934. It spanned the deep chasm made by the Colorado River, which had formed the Grand Canyon. In 1995 a new bridge was built, leaving the old one that we had crossed for pedestrians and horses. We drove along the South Rim of the Grand Canyon and found a campsite on the edge with a wonderful view of the Painted Desert with its varied colors of reds and lavenders.

AUGUST 24, DAY 24: A drive along the south rim of the canyon included stops to admire the views and take photos. Our destination was Wickenburg, near Phoenix, where we stayed at the Arizona home of Mark and Jean Bandy, whose farm in Iowa we had visited on our way out west. In 1958, soon after our visit, the Bandys retired to their Wickenburg home where Mark set up his mineral collection in a special building to be viewed by visitors and mineral collectors. The Bandys had kindly arranged for us to pick up the key to their house from the estate agent's office so we could make use of their lovely ranch house for a two-day break from camping. Mr. White, the estate agent, took us to the house and showed us how to turn on the water and electricity. It was bliss to stay in a beautiful home after so many weeks camping and a few motels. We began to taste civilized living, and looked forward to getting back to our home in State College. We took showers, did laundry, and explored the garden of cacti and interesting deserts plants, being careful to watch for snakes. The next day we declined Mr. White's offer of golf or sightseeing and explored the small town on our own. I had my hair cut and while our car was being fixed, we talked to the owner of a store that sold Indian jewelry, learning that handcrafts are dying out as Indians find jobs in industry. Mrs. Frick told us that much of the good jewelry is made by the Zuni tribe, and that during the war the Hopis believed that Hitler was a white brother who would come and restore their land. She explained that the Indians worship the sun, sometimes have two wives, and the women do most of the work. Mr. and Mrs. White invited us to their home for dinner, treating us to a western style barbecue.

Romy at the south rim of the Grand Canyon, Arizona

From Wickenburg, we drove to Gallup, New Mexico, with some breaks along the way. We visited a ghost town where a copper mine had been abandoned in 1953. It was a strange sensation to drive along the narrow, winding streets with boarded up stores and empty houses on the hillside above. After a stop in Flagstaff, where we had two new tires put on the car, we visited the Petrified Forest National Monument and admired the many tree stumps turned into rock with variegated colors made by traces of iron oxide. On the way, we drove through Albuquerque and Santa Fe where flags and decorations were being erected in preparation for a festival. We walked through the arcades around the central square and admired the variety of wares displayed on the sidewalk by Indian women. In New Mexico, our objective was to find the Harding Pegmatite Mine and meet up with geologists Dick Jahns and Wayne Burnham whom we had met at Penn State, and with whom Pete would have future academic connections. Our car struggled up a rough and extremely steep road, but we managed to find the mine. We enjoyed an evening supper at a ranch lodge and Pete talked geology with Dick, Wayne, and Art Montgomery, the owner of the mine. For most of the next day, Pete toured the mine while I wrote letters home. Before we left, Dick Jahns gave me a piece of gem-quality tourmaline from a mine near San Diego, California. Our visit to the mine had taken us through the back country of New Mexico, giving us a chance to see Native American villages scattered among large agricultural areas.

AUGUST 28, DAY 31: Our next stop was a campground in Questa in the Red River Valley, New Mexico, after paying a visit to the old Spanish town of Taos where we toured some art galleries, and the Taos Pueblo, an old Indian village. The pueblo is regarded as a sacred place by the Indians, some of whom still live there. It was several stories high with ladders accessing the different levels. Although it was probably to impress tourists like us, we were intrigued to see many of the Indians wearing national dress: women had shawls over their heads with long colorful dresses and moccasins, or trousers and boots; the men wore bandanas around their heads and towels tied at the waist over trousers.

AUGUST 29, DAY 32: gave us our first sight of the Rocky Mountains. They rose high and dauntless with snow patches visible near their peaks. Our drive took us through the old mining town of Leadville, Colorado, with many mines scattered over the hillsides. We climbed ever higher until we drove over the famous 11,998-foot Loveland Pass and the Continental Divide, where the water on one side goes to the Pacific Ocean and on the other side to the Atlantic Ocean. We spent the night at Stillwater Creek campsite, Granby Lake in the Rocky Mountain National Park where it was considerably cooler than in the lowlands of New Mexico. In the morning we climbed over Milner Pass and admired views of the valley below with the Colorado River, now just a little stream meandering along not far from its source. There were mountains all around, some with angular peaks well above the timber line. The Trail Ridge Road, the longest road in the U.S. at such a height, took us past Iceberg Lake to the highest point at 12,110 feet. We were awed by the spectacular views of the canyon far below and nearby peaks displaying patches of snow, canyons, colorful wild flowers, and alpine lakes shimmering in the bright sunlight. It was freezing cold and the wind was so strong that it broke the hinge of the car door as Pete got out to take a photograph. We were amused by the chipmunks, squirrels, and fat furry marmots who were tame enough to eat out of our hands. As we descended slowly to Estes Park and Boulder, the scenery changed to streams cutting through ravines followed by meadows. Soon we had a view of the great undulating plains spreading out from the foot of the Rockies. As we left with the Rockies rising up behind us, Route 36 took us across Colorado and into St. Francis, Kansas. On our drive across the great plains, we stopped near Lebanon to view a monument and small park marking the geographical center of the United States.

On our 34th day we reached the midwest, well on our way home to Pennsylvania. We crossed the wide and muddy Missouri River and camped for the night at Wallace State Park, near Cameron, Missouri. September 1, Labor Day, and our 35th day, was cool and stormy. We just managed to strike camp and get packed up before the storm hit with thunder, lightning, and pouring rain. We crossed over the Mississippi River at Hannibal and into Illinois where we camped at Turkey Run State Park, near Rockville. The following days were taken up with slow driving as we crossed Indiana and Ohio. The pre-Interstate roads were good but the towns had speed limits, and when we hit school traffic going home, buses and crazy teenagers driving cars delayed us.

SEPTEMBER 3, DAY 37: This was our last day on the road. We left a campsite in Blue Rock, near Zanesville, Ohio at 8:00 A.M. and reached State College, Pennsylvania at 6:00 P.M. Home at last, having driven 8,795 miles across America. Our car had made it but not without many headaches, mostly its inability to climb hills without the radiator boiling. Our Pontiac had required a new wheel to replace one that had been damaged in a previous accident, a water pump, a regulator, fan belt, two new tires, and many oil changes.

In spite of the discomforts and challenges of endless camping, the trip was an unforgettable undertaking: We had discovered the grandeur of the western states with such variable scenery and fascinating geology; we had camped in the National Parks, which were remarkable for their cleanliness, organization, and the helpfulness of the rangers; we had experienced first-hand the wild west that we had seen in movies and been impressed by the friendliness of the people; we had swum in the Pacific Ocean, and toured significant California cities. However, we were glad to get back to a civilized mode of living: a comfortable bed, showers every day, laundry facilities, and food that didn't consist of endless cans of baked beans or canned meats. Our plan for pregnancy had been successful. As many foods became unattractive, I knew that I was in the family way. We think that conception happened in our tilting tent in the Badlands.

12. FAREWELL

Will ye no' come back again?
Better lo'ed ye canna be
Will ye no' come back again?
—"Bonnie Charlie" by Carolina Oliphant

After a visit to a doctor, my pregnancy was confirmed. Our baby would be due in April 1959, about three months before our planned return to Great Britain. Recovering from our exciting western adventure, we both returned to our jobs. Fortunately, I had a straightforward pregnancy with some morning sickness, but nothing that interfered with work, although I kept dry crackers at my desk and took a dislike to coffee, both its smell and taste, and a stronger dislike to the smell of cigars, which our first-floor judge smoked all day long.

In October 1958, after learning the news of our expectancy, my medical father sent advice:

I would advise you to keep off alcohol especially gin and whisky, the latter I do trust you do not indulge in—it is a bad drink for women. You should be able to continue in your job well into the New Year. What does your doctor say? By the way, cut down smoking as much as you can. I hope you won't think I am trying to interfere, but I have had a very long experience. It is 39 years since I arrived in Hull as an Assistant Surgeon, and 47 years since I qualified.

This was excellent advice that today's expectant mothers follow much more rigorously than we did in 1958.

Pete continued his all-absorbing research with Professor Tuttle, and we continued to enjoy social life and athletic activities. We did start to think about preparing and packing for our return home. With every grocery shop, I had collected green stamps that I traded in for an exciting assortment of items. I chose to spend most of them on copper bottom pans and now had an attractive and serviceable collection of cookware. We had arrived in State College with two cabin trunks and two or three suitcases. As we started packing, we found it necessary to purchase more trunks ordered from Sears & Roebuck, the only respectable and our go-to department store in rural State College. Before long, we had obtained six more trunks. How had we acquired so much "stuff"?

Pete had been accepted for a Fellowship in Chemistry at the University of Leeds starting in September 1959. Our plan was to stay first with my family in Swanland, while Pete would go to Leeds to look for housing. My father had suggested that we consider buying a house rather than renting, and as we would have a baby, that was certainly our hope. I corresponded regularly with my parents. Mummy wrote warm loving letters weekly—Daddy wrote less often but just as tenderly. On December 17, 1958, he wrote to wish us a happy Christmas along with the following advice: "Take great care of yourself and I can assure you it is well worth it. I shall think of you at Christmas time and we shall drink to your health, and of course Peter's." He explained that Mummy felt Pete should be getting a higher salary than what had been offered at Leeds, but Daddy assured me that he understands these things more readily and would, "trust Pete to do what he considered to be the best objective for him."

We were so looking forward to seeing our families again and enjoying some of the English foods that we had missed, but it would be hard to leave all our new friends in State College. Our three years in America had been an extraordinary experience: Pete had done rewarding scientific research, and I had managed to adjust my British secretarial training to an unusual language and business practice; we had experienced a different culture and explored many of the vast territories of the United States; and most important of all, we had made lasting friendships. It would be difficult to say goodbye.

For our last Christmas and New Year in the US, we planned festive celebrations with our Penn State friends. On New Year's morning, as we were recovering from the previous evening's revelries, Pete received a telegram from my brother George with the devastating news that my father had died. Pete told me as gently as he could, but it was so sudden and so shocking. My father did have high blood pressure, but hadn't been seriously ill, although he had mentioned to me in his last letter, written on December 29, that: "I am having my second chill in four weeks and don't seem to throw it off easily."

When the National Health Service, funded out of general taxation, came into effect in 1948, my father's position as Senior Surgeon at the Hull Royal Infirmary was terminated. Because he hadn't been in the service long enough, he did not receive a pension. With a son still in boarding school, my father had to find work, so he did locums—standing in temporarily for another doctor—and at the time of his death was working half days for a Dr. Maude at Sutton. On the last day of 1958, he was driving to his job when he felt ill and turned his car around to return home. Hearing a car crash—it had swerved across the road and hit a lamp post—a woman, who had once been a patient of my father's, came out of her house and found him. He had lost consciousness, but was not injured in the crash. Daddy had suffered a cerebral hemorrhage at the relatively young age of 71. An ambulance rushed him to the Hull Royal Infirmary where he had done

Romy with Pete feeling their baby move

so much of his life's work, but it was too late. Nothing could be done, and he never regained awareness. Naturally, mother was distraught. My youngest brother, Bob, rushed home from his job at Blackburn & General Aircraft company and gave her as much moral support as he could, and my two older brothers, George and John—both were working in London—caught the first available train to Hull, arriving late afternoon.

I was numb with grief and recalled the premonition that I had experienced when I said goodbye to my father in Edinburgh three years ago and felt that I would never see him again. That foreboding had come true. And I had no chance to say a final farewell. Although I was only six months pregnant, we decided that it wouldn't be wise to travel to England for the funeral. We had come over by ship and expected to return by ship because flying was too expensive. A journey by ship would have taken over a week and was not something I felt able to do on my own. Instead, I wrote to mother, and we sent red roses for the coffin. George and John wrote letters with all the details of the service, cuttings from the newspapers, and an obituary published in the British Medical Journal, which included the following tribute by E. M. D.:

The sudden passing of Mr. R. B. Blair came as a very great shock to his many friends. He was always one who bore his years lightly and seemed to be full of energy and a desire to continue in active medicine. He was a first-class surgeon and showed his special skill in orthopedic work. He was particularly interested in treating orthopedic abnormalities in children.

He had been a freemason and president of the Hull Literary and Philosophical Society, as well as president of several local medical societies. The well-attended funeral service was held at All Saints Church in North Ferriby where we were married.

Somehow, I managed to pull myself together, keep going with my job and social life, exchanging many letters with Mother, focusing on the upcoming birth of our first child whom my father would never meet, and preparations for our return to Great Britain. All of us took comfort in the fact that Pete and I would soon be back home, bringing with us a new life to make up the one that had been lost.

JULY 2020: I began this story three months ago, soon after we had been ordered to stay home because of the coronavirus pandemic. With most activities—concerts, social events, medical and beauty appointments—cancelled, I have been able to immerse myself in writing my memoir. The many rules and regulations imposed on our lives to try and slow the spread of COVID-19 brought to mind similar restrictions affecting daily living during World War II. An idyllic childhood was quickly interrupted by the outbreak of war and the struggles that accompanied it. The book follows my life from childhood to boarding school to university to marriage to a three-year sojourn in America. *From There to Here* is a prequel to *Loving Andrew,* which tells the story of our first child's birth and subsequent parenting challenges, a few months before our return to England.

As I sit in my California home reminiscing about the places of my childhood like *The Land of Green Ginger Street*, the coronavirus pandemic is still in full swing around the globe with many months anticipated before a vaccine is developed and we can return to normal, or at least a new normal. Although we expect that the deadly disease will eventually be controlled, we must be patient, learn from all the necessary changes, and make the best of life, just as we survived six years of turmoil in the 1940s before the war ended and peace treaties were signed.

My father, Major Robert Bertram Blair, in his dress uniform of the Royal Army Medical Corps

SELECTED BIBLIOGRAPHY

BOOKS

Banks, Mike, Captain, Royal Marines. *High Arctic*. London:
J. M. Dent & Sons Ltd, 1957

Larson, Erik. *The Splendid and the Vile*. New York:
Penguin Random House LLC, 2020

Simpson, C. J. W., Commander, Royal Navy. *North Ice*.
London: Hodder and Stoughton, 1957

MISCELLANEOUS

Blair Family Archives. Correspondence, Newspaper Cuttings,
Photographs

Wyllie Family Archives. Diaries, Correspondence, Photographs

Sarjeant, Aileen A. *Can't Internment be Humanized?*
Unpublished Essay, 1941

University of St. Andrews. *Alumnus Chronicle*, 2009, 2011, 2012,
2013, 2015

University of St. Andrews. *Research at the Edge*, 2012

PHOTOGRAPHY CREDITS

ACKNOWLEDGEMENTS

Writing a book is never a solo journey. I wish to thank all the people, family, friends, teachers, and acquaintances who helped me grow, learn, and develop into the adult I am today. Many of them have passed on but, dead or alive, they are all part of this story. I wish to thank my cousin, Lolla Harrison, for allowing me to use her mother's unpublished essay on her concentration camp experience. My good friend Robin Richstone for granting me permission to reproduce her poem *The Land of Green Ginger*, and Chris Fowlie for allowing me to use the letter Pete wrote to her from Greenland. My sister-in-law, Margaret Blair, provided the photograph of my childhood home, and my brother John's son, Chris Blair, helped me with details of his father's occupation. I appreciate the comments and suggestions of my readers: husband Peter Wyllie, daughter Lisa Behm, son John Wyllie, friends Susan Grether, Marcia Hudson, Art Montana, and Lynn Rodriguez. My writer friend Beverly Russell, was consistently available with advice, ideas, and encouragement. My granddaughter-in-law, Nancy Behm, prepared the first round of editing and Lisa Rojany, Editorial Services of Los Angeles, completed a second round. My photographer friend, Steve Berg, who lives in Hawaii, achieved wonders with my archival photos. Elaine Cartwright, who works in the Alumni Office at the University of St. Andrews, helped me with permissions and arranged for me to use a photograph of the iconic pier walk. James Alexander of Jade Design, London worked his magic designing both the book's interior and cover. Finally, I wish to thank my dear husband, Pete, with whom I have shared my adult life and all its stages for the past 64 years.

BIOGRAPHY

Romy Wyllie is an honorary alumna of the California Institute of Technology where she co-founded and led an architectural tour service for thirty-three years. Wyllie had her own interior design business for thirty-five years and is a professional member of the International Interior Design Association. She is also a member of the Society of Architectural Historians, the Zamorano Club, and a reader at the Huntington Library. Wyllie began writing in her mid-sixties and has published four books: three on architecture and interior design, *Caltech's Architectural Heritage: From Spanish Tile to Modern Stone* (Balcony Press, Los Angeles 2000); *Bertram Goodhue: His Life and Residential Architecture,* (W. W. Norton, New York & London 2007); and a monograph on Interior Designer *Eva Maddox: Designer, Educator, Innovator* (Images Publishing Group, Australia 2017). In November 2012, Wyllie moved away from architectural histories to document the life of her son in *Loving Andrew: A Fifty-Two-Year Story of Down Syndrome.* This book has received eight awards. Wyllie has a Master of Arts degree from the University of St. Andrews, Scotland, and diplomas in Business Practices and Interior Design.

CPSIA information can be obtained
at www.ICGtesting.com
Printed in the USA
JSHW020012081220
10089JS00004B/11